CliffsNotes

Dip Ed,
and Gary K. Carey, M.A.

IN THIS BOOK

- Learn about the Life and Background of the Author

- Preview an Introduction to the Play

- Study a graphical Character Map

- Explore themes and literary devices in the Critical Commentaries

- Examine in-depth Character Analyses

- Reinforce what you learn with CliffsNotes Review

- Find additional information to further your study in the CliffsNotes Resource Center and online at www.cliffsnotes.com

Wiley Publishing, Inc.

Editor
Gary Carey, M.A., University of Colorado

Consulting Editor
James L. Roberts, Ph.D., Department of English, University of Nebraska

Publisher's Acknowledgments
Senior Project Editor: Michael Kelly
Acquisitions Editor: Greg Tubach
Copy Editor: Greg Pearson
Glossary Editors: The editors and staff at Webster's New World Dictionaries
Editorial Administrator: Michelle Hacker
Editorial Assistant: Brian Herrmann
Production
Wiley Publishing, Inc., Indianapolis Composition Services

CliffsNotes™ *Othello*

Published by:
Wiley Publishing, Inc.
909 Third Avenue
New York, NY 10022
www.wiley.com

Copyright © 2000 Wiley Publishing, Inc., New York, New York
Library of Congress Control Number: 00-104234
ISBN: 0-7645-8587-8
Printed in the United States of America
10 9 8 7 6 5 4
1O/QR/QW/QS/IN
Published by Wiley Publishing, Inc., New York, NY
Published simultaneously in Canada

Table of Contents

How to Use This Book

CliffsNotes *Othello* supplements the original work, giving you background information about the author, an introduction to the novel, a graphical character map, critical commentaries, expanded glossaries, and a comprehensive index. CliffsNotes Review tests your comprehension of the original text and reinforces learning with questions and answers, practice projects, and more. For further information on William Shakespeare and *Othello,* check out the CliffsNotes Resource Center.

CliffsNotes provides the following icons to highlight essential elements of particular interest:

Reveals the underlying themes in the work.

Helps you to more easily relate to or discover the depth of a character.

Uncovers elements such as setting, atmosphere, mystery, passion, violence, irony, symbolism, tragedy, foreshadowing, and satire.

Enables you to appreciate the nuances of words and phrases.

Don't Miss Our Web Site

Discover classic literature as well as modern-day treasures by visiting the CliffsNotes Web site at www.cliffsnotes.com. You can obtain a quick download of a CliffsNotes title, purchase a title in print form, browse our catalog, or view online samples.

You'll also find interactive tools that are fun and informative, links to interesting Web sites, tips, articles, and additional resources to help you, not only for literature, but for test prep, finance, careers, computers, and the Internet too. See you at www.cliffsnotes.com!

LIFE AND BACKGROUND OF THE AUTHOR

Many books have assembled facts, reasonable suppositions, traditions, and speculations concerning the life and career of William Shakespeare. Taken as a whole, these materials give a rather comprehensive picture of England's foremost dramatic poet. Tradition and sober supposition are not necessarily false because they lack proven bases for their existence. It is important, however, that persons interested in Shakespeare should distinguish between facts and beliefs about his life.

From one point of view, modern scholars are fortunate to know as much as they do about a man of middle-class origin who left a small country town and embarked on a professional career in sixteenth-century London. From another point of view, they know surprisingly little about the writer who has continued to influence the English language and its drama and poetry for more than three hundred years. Sparse and scattered as these facts of his life are, they are sufficient to prove that a man from Stratford by the name of William Shakespeare wrote the major portion of the thirty-seven plays that scholars ascribe to him. The concise review that follows will concern itself with some of these records.

Personal History

No one knows the exact date of William Shakespeare's birth. His baptism occurred on Wednesday, April 26, 1564. His father was John Shakespeare, tanner, glover, dealer in grain, and town official of Stratford; his mother, Mary, was the daughter of Robert Arden, a prosperous gentleman-farmer. The Shakespeares lived on Henley Street.

Under a bond dated November 28, 1582, William Shakespeare and Anne Hathaway entered into a marriage contract. The baptism of their eldest child, Susanna, took place in Stratford in May, 1583. One year and nine months later their twins, Hamnet and Judith, were christened in the same church. The parents named them for the poet's friends, Hamnet and Judith Sadler.

Early in 1596, William Shakespeare, in his father's name, applied to the College of Heralds for a coat of arms. Although positive proof is lacking, there is reason to believe that the Heralds granted this request, for in 1599 Shakespeare again made application for the right to quarter his coat of arms with that of his mother. Entitled to her father's coat of arms, Mary had lost this privilege when she married John Shakespeare before he held the official status of gentleman.

In May of 1597, Shakespeare purchased New Place, the outstanding residential property in Stratford at that time. Since John Shakespeare had suffered financial reverses prior to this date, William must have achieved success for himself.

Court records show that in 1601–1602, William Shakespeare began rooming in the household of Christopher Mountjoy in London. Subsequent disputes over the wedding settlement and agreement between Mountjoy and his son-in-law, Stephen Belott, led to a series of legal actions, and in 1612 the court scribe recorded Shakespeare's deposition of testimony relating to the case. In July, 1605, William Shakespeare paid four hundred and forty pounds for the lease of a large portion of the tithes on certain real estate in and near Stratford. This was an arrangement whereby Shakespeare purchased half the annual tithes, or taxes, on certain agricultural products from parcels of land in and near Stratford. In addition to receiving approximately 10 percent income on his investment, he almost doubled his capital. This was possibly the most important and successful investment of his lifetime, and it paid a steady income for many years.

Shakespeare is next mentioned when John Combe, a resident of Stratford, died on July 12, 1614. To his friend, Combe bequeathed the sum of five pounds. These records and similar ones are important, not because of their economic significance but because they prove the existence of William Shakespeare in Stratford and in London during this period.

On March 25, 1616, William Shakespeare revised his last will and testament. He died on April 23 of the same year. His body lies within the chancel and before the altar of the Stratford church. A rather wry inscription is carved upon his tombstone:

> Good Friend, for Jesus' sake, forbear
> To dig the dust enclosed here;
> Blest be the man that spares these bones
> And curst be he who moves my bones.

The last direct descendant of William Shakespeare was his granddaughter, Elizabeth Hall, who died in 1670.

These are the most outstanding facts about Shakespeare the man, as apart from those about the dramatist and poet. Such pieces of information, scattered from 1564 through 1616, declare the existence of such a person, not as a writer or actor, but as a private citizen. It is illogical to think that anyone would or could have fabricated these details for the purpose of deceiving later generations.

His Work

In similar fashion, the evidence establishing William Shakespeare as the foremost playwright of his day is positive and persuasive. Robert Greene's *Groatsworth of Wit*, in which he attacked Shakespeare, a mere actor, for presuming to write plays in competition with Greene and his fellow playwrights, was entered in the Stationers' Register on September 20, 1592. In 1594, Shakespeare acted before Queen Elizabeth, and in 1594–1595, his name appeared as one of the shareholders of the Lord Chamberlain's Company. Francis Meres in his *Palladis Tamia* (1598) called Shakespeare "mellifluous and hony-tongued" and compared his comedies and tragedies with those of Plautus and Seneca in excellence.

Shakespeare's continued association with Burbage's company is equally definite. His name appears as one of the owners of the Globe (a theater) in 1599. On May 19, 1603, he and his fellow actors received a patent from James I designating them as the King's Men and making them Grooms of the Chamber. Late in 1608 or early in 1609, Shakespeare and his colleagues purchased the Blackfriars Theatre and began using it as their winter location when weather made production at the Globe inconvenient.

Other specific allusions to Shakespeare and to his acting and his writing occur in numerous places. Put together, they form irrefutable testimony that William Shakespeare of Stratford and London was the leader among Elizabethan playwrights.

One of the most impressive of all proofs of Shakespeare's authorship of his plays is the First Folio of 1623, with the dedicatory verse that appeared in it. John Heminge and Henry Condell, members of Shakespeare's own company, stated that they collected and issued the plays as a memorial to their fellow actor. Many contemporary poets contributed eulogies to Shakespeare; one of the best known of these poems is by Ben Jonson, a fellow actor and, later, a friendly rival. Jonson also criticized Shakespeare's dramatic work in *Timber: or, Discoveries* (1641).

Certainly there are many things about Shakespeare's genius and career that the most diligent scholars do not know and cannot explain, but the facts that do exist are sufficient to establish Shakespeare's identity as a man and his authorship of the thirty-seven plays that reputable critics acknowledge to be his.

INTRODUCTION TO THE PLAY

Introduction

Shakespeare used existing stories as the basis for many of the plots of his plays. He took some from history (*Macbeth,* for example is based on Holinshed's *Chronicles*) and some from stories that were circulating in books at the time. Shakespeare's tragedy *Othello*, written and performed in 1604 and first printed in 1622, is based on a tale in Cinthio's *Hecatommithi* (1565), "Un Capitano Moro." What's interesting to modern readers is how Shakespeare adapted these stories, turning bare narratives into gripping drama.

The Original Story

The original tale, "Un Capitano Moro," concerns an unnamed Moor who marries a beautiful lady, Desdemona, despite her parents' opposition. The Moor and Desdemona live happily in Venice, and the Moor is appointed commander of troops sent to the garrison at Cyprus. He takes his wife with him.

The Moor's wicked ensign falls in love with his commander's wife, Desdemona. The ensign is afraid he will be killed if the Moor discovers his secret, and all his efforts to impress Desdemona go unnoticed because she only thinks of her husband. The ensign imagines that she loves someone else, a handsome young captain who is also in Venice, and his love turns to bitter hatred. He plots to kill the captain and revenge himself on Desdemona.

The ensign bides his time. He sees his opportunity when the Moor degrades the captain for wounding a soldier and Desdemona tries to make peace between her husband and the captain. The ensign hints that Desdemona has her own reason to want the captain reinstated. When his wife claims that the demotion was an overreaction, the Moor becomes very angry and suspects that his ensign had spoken truthfully. When the ensign tells the Moor that the captain told him of the affair, the Moor demands to see proof of it.

The ensign and his wife have a daughter aged about three, and one day when Desdemona visits their house, he puts the child on her lap. As Desdemona and the child play, the ensign steals one of her handkerchiefs. The ensign then leaves the handkerchief on the bed of the young captain, who recognizes it and goes to return it to Desdemona. When the Moor answers his knock at the door, the captain runs away, but not before the Moor recognizes him.

Later, the ensign laughs and jokes with the captain where the Moor can see them; he then tells the Moor him that he and the captain were talking about the captain's love affair with Desdemona and a handkerchief that she had given him. The Moor, believing that the handkerchief constitutes proof of his wife's infidelity, demands it of his wife, who, of course, cannot produce it. The Moor decides that he must kill his wife and plots with the ensign to kill both his wife and the captain.

The ensign, after a large payment, waylays the captain, attacks him with his sword, and manages to wound him on the leg. Desdemona is tearful to see the captain in pain, and the Moor and the ensign beat her to death with a sand filled stocking. Then they pulled down the rotten timber ceiling on her, making it appear that the falling roof had killed her. The Moor, distracted with grief for his dead wife, turns against the ensign and cashiers him.

The ensign now plots to ruin the Moor. He goes back to Venice with the captain, now one-legged, and they accuse the Moor of injuring him and murdering Desdemona. The Moor is arrested, refuses to speak under torture, and is banished and later killed by Desdemona's family. The ensign pursues his career of villainy with other victims, but in the end is arrested and dies under torture.

For a complete retelling of this story, see *The Arden Shakespeare: Othello,* edited by M. R. Ridley. London: Methuen, 1965.

Shakespeare's Version

In creating his tragedy *Othello,* Shakespeare tightened and drama-tized the original story in several ways. The plot is concentrated in time and space, other characters are introduced to give, in several places, a double motive for an action. Iago now plots to destroy Othello, for a variety of motives, rather than Desdemona. Roderigo provides Iago with a useful dupe; his existence allows Iago to outline his wicked plans in conversation rather than soliloquy and to demonstrate his capacity for ruthless manipulation. Emilia provides a running commentary on Iago and his character, which she ascribes to all men. She innocently picks up the handkerchief, allowing the elimination of the daughter from the plot, and is a quick source of the information that finally condemns Iago.

Shakespeare also significantly altered the story's ending, concentrat-ing revenge, love, and despair in the final dramatic scene of the play: murder in the marriage bed, followed immediately by revelation and grief. Shakespeare's Othello murders his wife alone, face to face, by strangulation, struggling with his love for her to the end.

By concentrating the action and developing the characters into fully realized human beings, with their own names, personalities, and ways of looking at the world, Shakespeare created a tragedy whose beauty and pathos is universal.

A Brief Synopsis

The play opens in the powerful city state of Venice, famous as a center of trade and banking and for its military might. It is in the early hours of the morning, and two men—Roderigo, a young gentleman and former suitor of Senator Brabantio's daughter Desdemona, and Iago, an ensign who claims to have been passed over for promotion by Othello—are outside Senator Brabantio's house to tell him the news of his daughter's elopement with Othello, the Moor.

After sharing the news of the secret marriage in words calculated to alarm him, the treacherous and vindictive Iago quickly departs, leaving Roderigo to confirm the story. Feigning friendship and concern, Iago then meets with Othello and tells him of Brabantio's reaction. Brabantio, Othello, and Desdemona appear before the Duke of Venice. Although Brabantio accuses Othello of seducing his daughter by witchcraft, Othello explains that he won Desdemona by telling her his adventures, and Desdemona, called to testify, convinces the senators that she has freely gone with Othello and married him for love.

The Duke appoints Othello as general of the defense forces against the Turks, and he must leave for Cyprus immediately. Desdemona requests permission to accompany Othello to Cyprus. With the Duke's permission, Othello arranges for Desdemona to follow him later in another ship with Iago, whom he mistakenly believes is a trusted friend, and Iago's wife, Emilia. Iago convinces Roderigo that Desdemona will soon tire of Othello and that he should follow her to Cyprus. To himself, Iago decides to make use of Cassio, the man he deeply resents and who received the promotion he himself wanted, as the instrument to destroy Othello.

In Cyprus, Iago plots against Othello, planting the seed of doubt about Desdemona's fidelity and implicating Cassio as her lover. Using Roderigo, Iago arranges a fight that ultimately results in Cassio's demotion. Believing that his chances of reinstatement are better if he has Desdemona plead his case to her husband, Cassio, with Iago's help, arranges for a private meeting with Desdemona, who promises to speak on his behalf to Othello until his reconciliation with Othello is achieved.

As Cassio leaves, Iago and Othello appear. Othello notices Cassio's speedy departure, and Iago quickly seizes the opportunity to point out that Cassio seems to be trying to avoid the Moor. Desdemona immediately and enthusiastically begins to beg Othello to pardon Cassio, as she promised, and will not stop her pleading until Othello, preoccupied with other thoughts, agrees. The moment Desdemona and Emilia leave, however, Iago begins to plant seeds of doubt and suspicion in Othello's mind.

Othello, beset by uncertainty and anxiety, later demands of Iago some proof that Desdemona is unfaithful. Using a handkerchief that Desdemona later innocently drops, Iago convinces Othello that she has been unfaithful, and he stages a conversation with the innocent Cassio that further hardens the Moor's heart against his wife and her supposed lover. Convinced of his wife's betrayal and enraged and grieving, Othello rushes into action, making an agreement with Iago that he, Othello, will kill Desdemona, and Iago will dispose of Cassio.

Desdemona, true to her word to Cassio, continues to plead on his behalf, unknowingly confirming to Othello her unfaithfulness. He accuses her of falseness, and Desdemona, not knowing what she has done to offend, can only assure him that she loves him.

Meanwhile, the gullible Roderigo has abandoned all hope of Desdemona, but Iago urges him to kill Cassio and rekindle his hopes. Late that night, they attack Cassio in the street, but it is Cassio who wounds Roderigo. Iago rushes out and stabs Cassio in the leg. Othello, hearing Cassio's cries for help, believes that half of the revenge is completed and hastens to fulfil his undertaking.

Desdemona is in bed when Othello enters. He tells her to pray a last prayer as he has no wish to kill her soul. Realizing that he plans to murder her, Desdemona protests her innocence of any wrongdoing. Knowing that he doesn't believe her, she begs him to let her live just a little longer, but he smothers her with a pillow.

Emilia, Desdemona's servant and Iago's wife, upon discovering the ruse, raises the alarm and declares Iago a liar before Montano and Gratiano. She explains how Desdemona's handkerchief came into Cassio's possession, and when she refuses to be quiet, Iago stabs her. Cassio, wounded, confirms Emilia's story. A soldier to the last, Othello stands on his honor. Knowing that this is the end, he asks to be remembered as "one that loved not wisely but too well." Then he stabs himself and falls on the bed beside his wife, where he dies.

List of Characters

Othello A Moor (an African), a general in the defense forces of the city state of Venice. His successful profession brings him high status in Venice, but his foreign origins and color separate him from those with whom he lives and works. He is a military man, with a reputation for courage in battle and good judgment in military matters. Othello falls in love and marries Desdemona, but during the campaign against the Turks, Othello is tricked by Iago into believing that his wife has been unfaithful with his lieutenant, Cassio. Iago works on Othello's personal and social insecurity until Othello believes the combination of Iago's lies and flimsy circumstantial evidence. Inflamed with jealousy, he smothers Desdemona in her bed, only to find out too late that he has been misled and has killed the woman who loved him faithfully. In despair, he kills himself.

Iago Othello's *ancient* (captain) in the Venetian defense forces. He had hoped for promotion, but Othello passed over him in favor of Cassio, and Iago works revenge on them both. He exploites Roderigo as a source of money and an unwitting accomplice in his plot to bring down Othello. When finally cornered and charged with his wickedness, Iago refuses to speak or to repent or explain his actions, and he goes to his punishment still surrounded by mystery.

Desdemona A noble Venetian lady, daughter of Brabantio. She organizes her life intelligently and shows courage, love, and loyalty in following her husband into danger. She accompanies Othello to Cyprus on the campaign against the Turks but finds him becoming distant and making wild accusations against her. She firmly believes that he will see that she is true to him, but when she realizes he is about to kill her, she can only feel despair and grief. She dies declaring her love for him.

Brabantio A Venetian Senator, Desdemona's father. He is angry at his daughter's choice of husband but can do nothing once the marriage has taken place, and the Venetian Senate has accepted it. He warns Othello that Desdemona is a clever deceiver.

Roderigo A Venetian nobleman in love with Desdemona. He has more money than sense and pays Iago to court Desdemona on his behalf. Iago, playing on Roderigo's hopes and gullibility, continues to help himself to Roderigo's money, and Roderigo never gets his heart's desire. Iago involves Roderigo in an attack on Cassio, for which Roderigo pays with his life, as Iago kills him to ensure his silence.

Cassio Othello's lieutenant in the Venetian defense forces. Cassio accompanied Othello as his friend when he was courting Desdemona. He is popular, he speaks well, and he is lively and trusting. Iago eventually convinces Othello that Cassio is Desdemona's paramour. Cassio is appointed governor of Cyprus after Othello's death.

Bianca A courtesan (prostitute), in love with Cassio. She is skilled in needlework and agrees to copy the handkerchief that Cassio gives her; then she throws it back at him, believing it is the token of his new love.

Emilia Desdemona's lady-in-waiting and Iago's wife. She knows Iago better than anybody else and is suspicious of his actions and motives. She does not realize until too late that the wicked person who has poisoned Othello against Desdemona is Iago, her own husband.

The Duke of Venice The leader of the governing body of the city state of Venice. The Duke appoints Othello to lead the forces defending Venice against the Turkish attack on Cyprus; he also urges Brabantio to accept his daughter's marriage.

Gratiano Brabantio's brother. He and Lodovico find Cassio wounded after Roderigo stabs him in the drunken brawl.

Lodovico Desdemona's cousin. After the death of Desdemona, Lodovico questions Othello and Cassio together, thus revealing the truth.

Montano Othello's predecessor as the governor of Cyprus. He is Othello's friend and loyal supporter.

Character Map

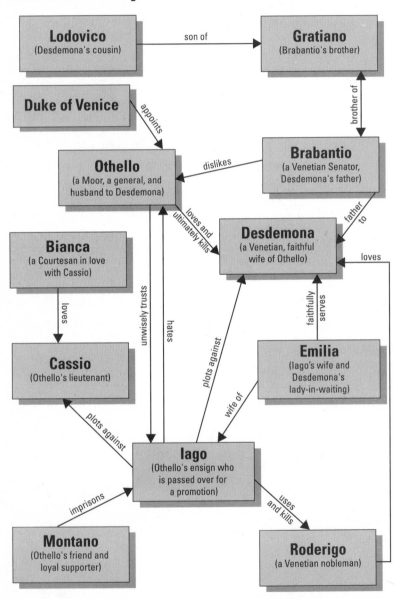

CRITICAL COMMENTARIES

Act I
Scene 1

Summary

On a street in Venice, there is an argument between Roderigo, a nobleman, and Iago, an *ancient* (captain) in the defense forces. Roderigo, in love with the noble lady Desdemona, has paid large sums of money to Iago, on the understanding that Iago would give her gifts from him and praise him to her. Roderigo hopes to win Desdemona's love and marry her. However, they now have news that Desdemona has left the house of her father, Brabantio, a Senator, and eloped with Othello, a Moor (an African) who is a General in the defense forces.

Roderigo fears he has lost both his lady and his money. Iago reveals to Roderigo that it is in his (Iago's) nature to plot and tell lies to get what he wants and that he has a plan. He hates Othello for promoting Cassio to the position of lieutenant, a position that Iago wanted for himself. Iago plans to bring about Othello's downfall, and Roderigo will have Desdemona. First, they must wake Brabantio and cause an outcry. They bang and shout until Brabantio comes out onto the balcony. Iago tells him in inflammatory words that Desdemona has run away with Othello, and Brabantio, enraged, joins Roderigo to wake the neighbors and organize a search party.

Commentary

The play begins with a quarrel of sorts between Iago and Roderigo, and, as such, it serves several functions. Its tone easily catches our interest, and it reveals Iago's wily nature; he must make amends to Roderigo for failing to arouse Desdemona's interest in him. After all, Iago intends to keep a hand in this wealthy nobleman's pocketbook, which, Roderigo says, belongs to Iago, "as if the strings were thine" (3). Iago apologizes profusely for failing Roderigo and claims that he never dreamed that such an elopement might occur: "If ever I did dream of such a matter," he says, "Abhor me" (5–6).

Exactly how long Iago has been capitalizing upon the gullibility of Roderigo, we do not know, but it is clear that Iago has no respect for Roderigo's intelligence. The guile he openly uses to stay in Roderigo's good stead is not even particularly crafty; blatantly, for example, he tells Roderigo, "I am not what I am" (65). Besides this statement being a capsule condemnation of Iago, it serves to point out that Roderigo *trusts* this man. Thus Roderigo gains a measure of our pity; he is a weak figure, probably victimized by everybody, not only in this matter of deceit.

Character
Insight

Far more important, however, than catching our interest and establishing Iago's basic character, this opening scene sets forth the key elements of the tragedy's conflict: It reveals Iago's deep resentment toward Othello. There are at least a couple of interpretations of Iago's feelings toward Othello. One is that Iago had expected to be promoted to the rank of Othello's first lieutenant and tells Roderigo that three influential Venetians ("Three great ones of the city"), in fact, had recommended him to Othello. Instead, Othello chose Cassio, a man, Iago tells Roderigo, whose military ineptitude is an insult to Iago's proven superiority on the battlefield. The other interpretation is that Iago was never in contention for the position and that he makes up this entire set of circumstances including the unnamed "great ones" in order to convince Roderigo of his hate for Othello. This argument is bolstered by the facts that none of the other characters, including Othello and Emilia (Iago's wife), ever mention or allude to these facts, and, indeed, Iago never mentions them again.

Iago further points out to Roderigo that Cassio, the newly appointed lieutenant, is not a true soldier. He is not even a Venetian, Iago says, but, of course, neither is Othello. Cassio is a Florentine, Iago reminds Roderigo, which is a damning epithet condemning the city's reputation as being a collection of financiers and bookkeepers. What knowledge Cassio has of the battlefield, according to Iago, he gained from textbooks; in other words, he is a student, not a practitioner of battle. Even a spinster, Iago says, knows more of the "division of a battle" (23) than this "bookish theoric" (24). Compare this assessment of Cassio's military ability with the one Iago gives when he is talking to Montano, "He [Cassio] is a soldier fit to stand by Caesar / And give direction" (II, iii, 122).

Iago rankles at being Othello's *ancient*—that is, his ensign. Furthermore, there is nothing Iago can do about the situation: "there's no remedy" (35). He realizes that "preferment goes by letter and affection" (36) and not by "old gradation" (37) (the traditional order of society).

But he will continue to appear to "serve" Othello so that eventually he can "serve [his] turn upon him" (42). Iago, however, is not bent on mere revenge. The extent and depth of his hate for Othello and his desire and willingness to totally destroy him require a motivation more compelling than having been passed over for this promotion. That motivation lies in the racial attitudes identified in the conversations, references, and defamatory images of the characters in this scene. This hatred for Othello *consumes* Iago, yet his motivations are less important to the plot and themes of the plan than the outcomes of his evil manipulations. In this scene, Iago reveals himself to Roderigo and the audience as a self-seeking, malicious individual who will use every device in order to attain his "peculiar end" (60).

Style & Language

Roderigo is the first to surface this racist attitude when he refers to Othello as "the thick-lips" (66); then, Iago, unsatisfied with Roderigo's ability to incense Brabantio, refers to Othello as "an old black ram" (88) who "is tupping your white ewe" (89) (Desdemona), "a Barbary horse" (111) and "the lascivious Moor" (126). And finally, in this scene, after having told Roderigo that he is not a welcome suitor for Desdemona, Brabantio learns that his daughter has eloped with Othello and says to Roderigo, "O, that you had had her!" Brabantio's sudden preference for Roderigo, who has already been proven somewhat a fool over Othello, has no obvious or logical base now or at anytime in the play other than the continually implied racism.

We learn that Brabantio has warned Roderigo "not to haunt about my doors" (96); "my daughter is not for thee" (98). Thus another dimension of this situation presents itself. Roderigo is not just a rich, lovesick suitor who is paying Iago good wages to further his case with the senator's daughter. Roderigo has been rejected by Brabantio as a candidate for Desdemona's hand—a fact that offers an interesting parallel: Iago has been denied his chance to become Othello's lieutenant, and Roderigo has been denied his chance to become a recognized suitor of Desdemona. Rejection and revenge, then, are doubly potent ingredients in this tragedy.

Character Insight

Iago is quick to realize that the timid Roderigo will never sufficiently raise the ire of Desdemona's father and, for this reason, he interrupts his patron and heaps even more insults on Othello. Yet—and this fact is important—Iago has *still* not named Othello as being the culprit, as being the man who kidnapped Desdemona and eloped with her. For example, Iago shouts out that Desdemona, at this moment, is being mounted by a "Barbary horse" (112). Brabantio's nephews, he says, will neigh, and, likewise, Brabantio's cousins will be "gennets" (113) (black Spanish horses). Still, however, he has not identified Othello by name; nor does he stress that it is Venice's *General Othello* who has absconded with Brabantio's daughter. This neglect on Iago's part—his failing to identify Othello—is dramatically important. Because Brabantio seems dense and uncomprehending, Iago can continue to curse Othello's so-called villainous nature and, thereby, reveal to the audience the depths of his (Iago's) own corruptness.

Literary
Device

Iago's brazen assertions and Roderigo's timorous apologies for awakening Brabantio are finally effective. Brabantio comprehends what Iago and Roderigo are saying and, in fact, recalls a dream that foretold of just such a calamity. Dreams and omens of this sort are common in literature of this time and create the sense that fate somehow has a hand in the tragic events about to follow.

As Brabantio moves into action, calling for more lights and arousing members of his household, Iago steals away, but not before explaining his reasons for doing so: It must not be public knowledge that Iago himself is an enemy of Othello; if Iago's machinations are to be successful, he must outwardly "show out a flag and sign of love, / Which is indeed but sign" (157–158). Thus he will manage to stay in Othello's good graces. For this reason, he must go and rejoin his general.

Character
Insight

In addition to this speech reminding us of Iago's dangerous, diabolical treachery, it also serves to inform us about Othello's significance to Venice. Othello is a superior public figure, one who will soon be summoned to end the Cyprian wars and a man upon whom the Venetian state depends for its safety. This fact is contained in Iago's comment that "another of his fathom they have none / To lead their business" (153–154). Othello is a man of high position, as well as one of high honor and one who is, therefore, worthy of being considered a tragic hero.

Glossary

(Here and in the following glossary sections, difficult words and phrases, as well as allusions and historical references, are explained.)

'sblood (4) [Obsolete] *euphemism for* by God's blood; used as an swearword.

bookish theoric (24) the student, not practitioner.

affined (39) [Obsolete] under obligation; bound.

cashiered (48) dismissed (but not necessarily without honor).

trimmed (50) [Obsolete] dressed up.

peculiar (60) private.

compliment extern (63) outward appearance.

daws (65) jackdaws or crows; here, fools.

thick-lips (66) the Moor.

Zounds (86) [Archaic] by God's wounds.

distemp'ring draughts (99) intoxicating drinks.

grange (106) an isolated farmhouse.

gennets for germans (113) Spanish for relatives.

accident (142) an occurrence.

Sagittary (158) the name of an inn.

deserve (183) reward.

Act I
Scene 2

Summary

Iago warns Othello that there may be a legal attempt to break the marriage, but Othello knows his military worth to Venice and meets the Duke and Senators with confidence. Cassio has been sent to fetch him to an urgent meeting about the situation in Cyprus. Iago tells Cassio of Othello's marriage. Brabantio's party arrives; Brabantio threatens Othello with violence and accuses him of using sorcery to seduce Desdemona, his reasoning being that she would never marry Othello voluntarily. Brabantio calls for Othello's arrest and imprisonment but cedes precedence to the Duke's summons to the emergency meeting.

Commentary

Othello is confident and happy, sure that his military standing will protect him from Brabantio's personal anger: "Let him do his spite. / My services which I have done the Signiory / Shall out-tongue his complaints" (18–20). Othello declares himself a free man, with royal ancestors (22), who would not compromise that freedom by marriage except to Desdemona.

When Brabantio's party arrives and Brabantio threatens him with his sword, Othello, surrounded by people who know and value him, deflects him with a show of courtesy and respect to the older man. In contrast, Brabantio's accusations are raw and direct: "Oh thou foul thief, where hast thou stowed my daughter?" (61–62).

Character Insight

Othello's first appearance on stage is as a man confident and in control of his life, calmly and deftly putting Brabantio's anger aside. This scene shows two strands of Shakespeare's plot developing at the same time: Othello's private life, where his marriage is soon to become public knowledge, and the political crisis with the threatened attack by the Turks, where he anticipates being sent to war in a commanding position. Othello is the powerful key figure in both stories; a man to be admired. In contrast to this intellectually powerful first impression, the audience confronts Othello as a visual spectacle: a black face surrounded by white faces, some of which are characters known to be hostile to him. On the intellectual level, one looks up to Othello, while on the emotional level, one wonders already whether he can manage to survive.

Glossary

yerked (5) stabbed.

signiory (18 here, the Venetian government.

siege (22) rank.

unhoused (26) unrestrained.

perfect soul (31) stainless conscience.

Janus (33) the two-faced god of the Romans.

galleys (40) officers of the galleys.

carack (50) large trading ship.

gross in sense (72) perfectly clear.

attach (77) arrest.

inhibited (79) [Rare] prohibited; forbidden.

inclining (82) party; side.

Act I
Scene 3

Summary

Several reports have come in from Cyprus, all calling attention to a Turkish fleet that is expected to attack. The reports differ in the size of the fleet, but all speak of the danger as the combined force has turned back toward Cyprus. Othello enters the meeting with Cassio, Brabantio, Iago, and others, and the Duke immediately appoints Othello to lead the forces to defend Cyprus.

At this point, the Duke notices Brabantio, who believes that his daughter has been corrupted with magic potions because, according to him, she wound never willingly marry such a man as she did. Initially, the Duke promises him support in a prosecution for witchcraft, a capital crime, against the man who has seduced his daughter, but when the Duke realizes the seducer is Othello, he calls on the general to defend himself.

Othello describes his courtship of Desdemona in a dignified and persuasive speech (76–93 and 127–169) and asks the Duke to send for Desdemona so that she may speak. Iago leads the group that goes to fetch her. When Othello finishes speaking, the Duke declares in favor of Othello: "I think this tale would win my daughter too" (170). Desdemona then speaks, gently outlining an argument so strong that it finishes the whole debate: She owes obedience and thanks to her father for her upbringing, but now that she is married, her loyalty is to her husband, just as her mother's loyalty was to Brabantio. Fathers must give way to husbands.

Othello must go immediately to Cyprus to command its defense, and Desdemona requests to go as well. The Duke grants her wish, and Othello, who must leave that night, delegates Iago to follow later in another ship, bringing Desdemona and whatever else is needed. Iago's wife, Emilia, will look after Desdemona as her maid. As Othello leaves. Brabantio warns Othello, "She has deceived her father, and may thee" (289), but Othello is certain of Desdemona's faithfulness.

Iago and Roderigo are left on stage. Roderigo is downcast and talks of drowning himself. Iago replies with scorn that such misery is silliness and convinces Roderigo to go to Cyprus and wait for Desdemona to come to him, as she will surely soon become bored with Othello. Iago, because he hates Othello, says he will help Roderigo have Desdemona and reminds Roderigo to bring plenty of money.

Iago, alone on stage, considers the situation: He has consolidated his source of money, and he has heard a rumor that Othello has had sex with his wife, Emilia. Although he does not believe the rumor, he will act as though he does to feed his hatred. Also Iago will aim to get Cassio's position of lieutenant, which he thinks should have come to him.

Commentary

During the military discussion, the audience discovers that Cyprus is of supreme value to the Venetians, and it is vital that it remain under Venetian control for protection of sea trade. Therefore, when command is conferred on Othello, the Duke is making a public statement that Venice relies on him completely. Othello rightly feels confident; whatever his marriage arrangements, he knows that the Senators will back him because they need him.

After they deal with the military crisis, the Senators consider how to avenge an injustice done to one of their members: Brabantio. By the time he arrives at the emergency meeting, Brabantio's rage has turned to grief, and the Senators treat Brabantio's grief as a personal loss, rather than a public matter. They think his daughter must have died, and, for Brabantio, it is as if she *had* died. He believes that she has so gone against nature that witchcraft must be to blame. The Duke, speaking with sympathetic indignation, promises Brabantio that he shall judge the offender, even if it were the Duke's own son: "the bloody book of law / You shall yourself read in the bitter letter / After your own sense" (68–69). This declaration is significant because witchcraft was a capital crime; the law on this topic was indeed "bloody" dealing with how a witch was to be tortured and eventually executed. Yet the Duke's rash promise to Brabantio immediately rebounds when Brabantio points to Othello: "Here is the man: this Moor" (71). Suddenly the commander appointed to save Venice from her enemies is under risk of execution. The Senate risks losing a war to satisfy one man's desire for revenge, so the Duke hopes that Othello can justify his actions.

Othello's defense speech is in two parts: the first (76–93) establishes him as a soldier successful in the service of Venice and respectful of the great men of the city, and the second (127–169) describes how stories of his adventures won Desdemona's interest and then her love.

Othello begins with words of respect for the Senate; "Most potent, grave, and reverend signiors, / My very noble and approved good masters" (76–77) and then acknowledges the obvious: He has married Brabantio's daughter. He declares he is a soldier with no skill in making speeches: "Rude am I in my speech / And little blessed with the soft phrase of peace" (81–82). This is an extraordinary declaration, appearing as it does within a very dignified and elegantly expressed speech that shows that Othello does indeed know how to express himself. Othello's elegant speeches come at psychologically important moments in his life: When he is under pressure, he summons up his strength, faces his situation, and presents his case in beautifully expressed images. The ability to compose himself and to give a speech under pressure has been a valued quality in a military leader. Othello uses that military ability here in defense of his private life.

Othello fills in the background: he has been a soldier in the field from the age of seven until nine months ago, when he came back to Venice. He says: "I will a round unvarnished tale deliver / Of my whole course of love" (90–91), round being a natural shape, like a stone or an apple, and unvarnished, without ornamentation. As he is charged with using magic, he will tell what magic he used, knowing that he used none.

Literary Device

At this point Shakespeare breaks off Othello's awaited speech for Brabantio's reflections on Desdemona and a discussion of court procedure. By making the audience wait once again to hear how the lady was won, Shakespeare increases the tension, making Othello's final speech all the more impressive.

Brabantio is not the first father to have an unrealistic view of his daughter and to be shocked when she seeks a lover or a husband that does not meet his image or expectations. He assumes with no evidence that a black face is "what she feared to look on" (98). He is blinded by his own prejudices, and he ascribes them to Desdemona, painting the picture of a daughter who could not possibly fall in love with a black man. His reasoning here seems to go thusly: racially mixed, intimate relationships are evil and entered into by good people through witchcraft; his daughter is good and shares his views; therefore, she was forced into this relationship with Othello by witchcraft.

The Duke responds with relief, recognizing that Brabantio's evidence is tenuous and that he has produced no actual proof of witchcraft. He sees Brabantio's evidence as "thin habits (insubstantial outward appearances) and poor likelihoods" (108). The Senator follows this up with a direct question: Did Othello use witchcraft to win the lady's love, or did he court her in the usual way, "as soul to soul" (113)?

All attention is now on Othello, who introduces his defense with endearing simplicity: "So justly to your grave ears I'll present / How I did thrive in this fair lady's love, / And she in mine." Othello explains that, when Brabantio invited him into his house, he would have a glimpse of family life in a cultured Venetian household, a strong contrast with the rough and ready life of a soldier on campaign. Brabantio put him at his ease and encouraged him to speak of his life and adventures. Although Othello has said that he cannot speak easily, it is as a speaker that Brabantio and his daughter appreciated him.

Style & Language

Othello tells the story of his life. A fighter since his early years, he was "taken by the insolent foe / And sold to slavery" (136). Shakespeare makes Othello's story rich in visual detail, but he distorts geographic facts for dramatic effect. Slave trading was part of general trade along the shipping routes of East and North Africa, and many slaves were sold in markets in the cities of the Middle East. Othello was redeemed from slavery—by whom and for what reason are not revealed—and was left far from his homeland, facts which probably contributed to his career choice as a professional soldier. Othello also describes his adventures fighting on sea and land.

Othello's speech helps us—and the Senators—understand why Desdemona has fallen in love with him. He capably presents to the Duke and the others a portrait of himself as a man who has spent almost all of his life in the field as a successful, active soldier. He asserts that Desdemona would hear these stories and she would "devour up my discourse" (149). Then, Othello explains, following an intimate tale of "some distressed stroke / That my youth suffer'd" (157–158) and bringing her to tears weeping in sympathy at stories so strange and pitiful, she declared that "she wish'd / That heaven had made her such a man" (162–163). Desdemona's intention is clear in telling Othello that his story could win her love: "[I]f I had a friend that lov'd her, I should but teach him to tell my story, and that would woo her" (164–166). This is a transparently disguised declaration of her love for him and her encouragement for his proposal.

This description of Desdemona, depicting a young woman who knows exactly what she wants and reaches out for it, contrasts markedly with Brabantio's fond notion of a quiet, still small daughter. Othello knows what she will say and speaks confidently and directly: "Here comes the lady, let her witness it" (170). Even before Desdemona speaks, it is clear that Othello has successfully defended himself when the Duke says: "I think this tale would win my daughter too" (171). Brabantio is stunned by the Duke's revelation and attempts to buttress his position when he remarks, "If she confess that she was half the wooer, / Destruction on my head, if my bad blame / Light on the man!" (176) In fact, Brabantio does not put the pertinent question to her. He retreats to a more formal position and asks her to whom she owes most obedience. This question places the debate in the abstract realm of perceptions and customs about the proper relationship between young women and the men in their lives. Brabantio can expect that the Senators will side with fathers in matters of disobedient daughters and that their opinion will turn to his advantage.

Considering that the play is set approximately in the late sixteenth century, Desdemona's defense of her actions is remarkably forthright, spirited, and courageous. Her ten brief lines are models of concise rationale. Hers, she says, was and is a "divided duty": She remains bound to her noble father for her "life and education"; he remains her "lord of duty," and she will always honor him as such. Now, however, she has a husband, and she will give all her loyalty to her husband, just as her mother gave her loyalty to Brabantio. "And so much duty as my mother show'd / To you, preferring you before her father, / So much I challenge, that I may profess, / Due to the Moor my lord" (186–188). In other words, fathers must give way to husbands.

Desdemona's argument, which sweeps personal matters into general principles, carries the day, and Brabantio abandons his accusation. He does not concede that he was wrong, only that he cannot answer it. He never puts to question her participation in the courtship or the matter of witchcraft, which was his original accusation. Nor does he ask her how she could marry a man whom he thinks should disgust her. Simply he gives up, "I have done" (189 and 198) and abandons Desdemona and the whole idea of fatherhood. Brabantio's stubbornness is an integral part of his personality. He is not a fool, however: He is a man who is losing power, and there is no way he can accommodate that loss while retaining his self respect. The Duke's attempts at conciliation fall on deaf ears.

Desdemona, having embarked on marriage with Othello, wishes to accompany him into the field of war as a faithful wife. " . . . [I]f I be left behind, / A moth of peace, and he go to the war, / The rites for which I love him are bereft me, / And I a heavy interim shall support, / By his dear absence. Let me go with him" (255–259). The word "dear" here means "closely felt." Desdemona longs to be with her husband, for the rites of marriage, for sexual intimacy, and she finishes with a direct request: let me go with him. The directness of this request takes even Othello by surprise. Of course he wants his wife with him, and for the same reasons, and he supports her request, expressing it in a more socially acceptable manner: " . . . I therefore beg it not / To please the palate of my appetite, / Nor to comply with heat, . . . But to be free and bounteous of her mind" (261–265).

The Duke tells Othello that he can make what arrangements he likes. The important thing is that he must leave this very night because "th' affair calls [for] haste" (277). Desdemona is somewhat taken aback by this order. But notice the Moor's reply: He loves her "with all [his] heart" (279). Truly, as the Duke notes to Brabantio, Othello "is far more fair than black" (291). Immediately, there remains only for the Moor to leave some trusted officer behind, one who will see that Desdemona is brought to Cyprus safely. Tragically, Othello chooses the very man whom he can trust least in all the world—"honest Iago" (295).

Literary Device

Brabantio is crushed; he is a defeated man who realizes that the Moor neither stole nor bewitched his daughter. However, he will never understand how his "jewel" (195) renounced all his paternal guidance and secretly married a man of a different race and nation. He leaves with a parting warning to Othello: "Look to her, Moor, have a quick eye to see: / She has deceiv'd her father, may do thee." (292–293). These last words to Othello in this scene are important. They are packed with irony and provide, in part, an example of dramatic presaging. Desdemona does not deceive Othello, but before long Othello will be so convinced that she has deceived him that he will murder her. Othello's reply to Brabantio is likewise ironic: He vows, "my life upon her faith!" (295). Shortly, he will take his own life because of his lack of faith in her faith—in her innocent, chaste fidelity.

In a soliloquy that ends the act, Iago introduces a second motive for his hatred of Othello; he says that it is common gossip that the Moor "'twixt my sheets . . . [has] done my office" (393–394) and, for Iago, "mere suspicion . . . will do . . . for surety" (395–396). It need hardly be pointed out here that we are listening to a man whose mind is poisoned. There is not the slightest bit of evidence anywhere in this play to indicate that Othello has had an affair with Emilia. Iago also reveals his next malicious plan of action. Aware that Othello trusts him, he will convince the Moor that Cassio is "too familiar" (402) with Desdemona. Othello, he says, "is of a free and open nature" (405); precisely, in Iago's words, Othello is an "ass"—naive, in other words, and we recall that Othello himself has already admitted that he knows "little of this great world . . . [except that which] pertains to feats of broils and battle" (86–87). In the final couplet, which contains the reference to "hell and night" (409) and to "monstrous birth" (410), we sense Iago rubbing his hands in glee; we see all too clearly the unnaturalness and the diabolical elements of his plans to destroy the union of Othello and Desdemona.

The witchcraft accusation raises the question, What constitutes evidence and proof of wrongdoing and what does not? Othello survived an accusation made by a man who believed the facts supported his accusation, simply because his inflamed prejudices allowed him no other possible explanation. Brabantio made the accusation of witchcraft against Othello with no solid evidence, and on the basis of Desdemona's testimony the charge was dismissed. Later in the play, Othello will commit the same error incited much for the same reasons by making a baseless accusation with equal conviction that he is right.

Othello defends himself against Brabantio's accusation by personal statement and by calling Desdemona to testify. This strategy saves him from the false condemnation. Yet later in the play, as he accuses Desdemona without specifying the accusation until too late, he will deny her the opportunity to speak to defend herself or to call on Cassio to testify. Othello, blinded by emotion, has not learned from his own experience, and the consequences will be disastrous.

Style & Language

Act I, Scene 3 is the first of the very long scenes, where much detailed development happens. Event after event is presented in quick succession, giving the impression of accelerated movement and excitement. Time in *Othello* is presented as passing very quickly, but a careful examination shows almost no markers to indicate what day it is or how each scene relates to the others in terms of time. There are three such long scenes in *Othello*: this one; Act III, Scene 3, in which Iago makes Othello jealous; and Act V, Scene 2, which contains the murder and explanations. Their emotional intensity structurally unites the drama.

In Europe between the fourteenth and the end of the eighteenth centuries, three unity issues for drama were developed and debated, based on Aristotle's "Unity of Action" theory: (1) *unity of time,* meaning that all the episodes or actions happen within very close time frame of a day or so; (2) *unity of place,* meaning the episodes or actions happen near or in close proximity to each other; and (3) *unity of action,* meaning each episode or action relates to episodes and actions preceding and following it. These unity issues never became rules or standards that playwrights had to or did particularly follow, but they were known and may help the reader understand the relationship of the scenes in Othello.

Glossary

composition (1) consistency.

jump (5) agree.

article (11) substance.

assay (18) a test.

in false gaze (19) looking the wrong way.

brace (24) stance of defense.

Ottomites (33) Turks.

restem (37) steer again.

frank appearance (38) no attempt to conceal.

engluts (57) [Archaic] devours.

mountebanks (61) charlatans who sell quack medicine.

rude (81) unpolished.

credit (97) reputation.

portance (139) [Archaic] one's bearing or demeanor; behavior.

anters (140) [Archaic] caves.

idle (140) barren.

Anthropophagi (144) man-eaters; cannibals.

grise (200) a degree or step.

fortitude (222) fortification.

besort (238) suitable company.

quality (251) profession.

a moth of peace (256) A useless creature living a luxurious life.

defend (266) forbid.

indign (273) [Obsolete] unworthy.

hyssop (323) a fragrant herb.

sequestration (347) separation.

coloquintida (351) a bitter fruit.

plume up (396) to gratify.

Act II
Scene 1

Summary

Act II and all subsequent acts take place in Cyprus, in the Venetian fortifications. Montano, Governor of Cyprus, awaits the arrival of the Venetian forces, delayed by a violent storm at sea. A messenger arrives with news that the Turkish fleet has been so damaged by the storm that it no longer threatens Cyprus. Cassio's ship, followed by Desdemona's ship, is the first Venetian ship to arrive. Desdemona's first question is for news of Othello. The two pass the time, waiting for news, and Iago watches, planning to catch Cassio in his own courtesies.

Othello finally arrives, triumphant, and he, Desdemona, and the others go into the fortress. Iago stays behind to tell Roderigo that Desdemona is in love with Cassio and convince him to pick a fight with Cassio to cause mutiny and have him removed. Iago, in his second soliloquy, speaks again of his hatred for Othello. The details are not yet clear, but Iago plans to drive Othello mad.

Commentary

An undefined length of time has elapsed since the scenes in Act I, during which Othello has set sail for Cyprus in one ship, Cassio in another, and Iago, Emilia, and Desdemona in a third. The ships arrive one by one, allowing the arriving members to talk about Othello while waiting for his arrival. Cassio describes to Montano Othello's new wife, Desdemona, with respect and a little awe as "our great captain's captain" (74). His elaborate tones underline both his education and the high expectations many have of benefits on all sides from Othello: "That he may bless this bay with his tall ship, / Make love's quick pants in Desdemona's arms, / Give renewed fire to our extinct spirits" (79–82).

Desdemona, Emilia, and Iago play word games, which show Iago's cynical view of women: " . . . you are pictures out of doors, / Bells in your parlours, wild-cats in your kitchens, / Saints in your injuries, devils being offended, / Players in your housewifery, and housewives in your beds" (108–111). That is, women are models of propriety when they go out, sweet conversationalists with guests, and angry spitfires to their servants. They claim to always be the injured party, fly into a rage at an adverse comment and are idle in matters of housework and penny-pinching with their sexual favors. Iago speaks bluntly, disparaging women, and Desdemona, along with everyone else, makes allowances for the rough speech of "honest" Iago. For balance, Emilia gives a cynical woman's view of men in Act V.

Style & Language

Iago meanwhile watches Cassio, seeking a weakness that he can exploit. He decides to focus on his courteous manners and attentions to Desdemona. " . . . With as little web as this will I ensnare as great a fly as Cassio. Ay, smile upon her, do. I will gyve thee in thine own courtship" (164–165). Shakespeare uses the break in rhythm—from poetry to prose, or visa versa—to denote emphasis or a change in mood. Note Iago switches from the cynically playful tone of the rhymed couplet in the colloquy to the serious prose in the aside.

The reunion of Othello and Desdemona is a happy celebration of their love. Othello greets Desdemona as his equal, his "fair warrior" (174). He has gone through Hell in the tempest and is now in Heaven with his wife and realizes that this is the happiest moment of his life: "If it were now to die, / 'Twere now to be most happy; for I fear / My soul hath her content so absolute / That not another comfort like to this / Succeeds in unknown fate" (181–184). There is also a dark side to his happiness, for he feels that the future cannot match it. Desdemona, however, looks forward—"our loves and comforts should increase, / Even as our days do grow" (186–187).

Literary Device

In an aside, Iago remarks that Othello is now "well tuned" (191) like a lute or guitar and sings sweetly, but Iago will "set down the pegs" (192), loosening the strings and spoiling the music, "As honest as I am" (193). Others, especially Othello, use the word "honest" in earnest when talking of Iago; Iago, however, uses it ironically. This use of an aside links Iago with stage villains in traditional forms of theatre, masques, pantomimes, and puppet shows.

Iago pushes Roderigo in an emotional stampede, overwhelming his idealized view of Desdemona with a flood of disparaging words, abusing her virtue, and besmirching her reputation. He sweeps aside Roderigo's protestations of her virtue: "Blest fig's end! (an obscene oath, a "fig" is the head of a penis) / The wine she drinks is made of grapes" (238), meaning she is just the same as ordinary women. He claims

Cassio is already courting her: "They met so near with their lips that their breaths embraced together" (239–245). Iago batters Roderigo with the sheer volume of his abuse until the weak gentleman agrees to do as he is told in the plot to disgrace Cassio. Then Iago, alone on stage, speaks his thoughts.

Iago's second soliloquy is very revealing. It shows him shaping a plan out of the confusion of his emotionally charged thoughts. Iago examines his own thoughts, especially his hatred for Othello: "The Moor, howbeit that I endure him not" (269) and finds a common thread in the "poisonous mineral" of jealousy that still swirls around the rumor that Othello has enjoyed Emilia. Iago could get his revenge by seducing Desdemona: "Now I do love her too . . . / But partly led to diet my revenge, / For that I do suspect the lusty Moor / Hath leaped into my seat, the thought whereof / Doth like a poisonous mineral gnaw my inwards" (272–278). Iago uses the word "love" here in a very cynical way, making it a combination of lust and power seeking. At first he sees his seduction of Desdemona as his revenge: "Till I am evened with him, wife for wife" (280). Then Iago realizes that the unsubstantiated jealousy that torments him is the very weapon he can use against Othello, who will be even more susceptible. Iago will lead Othello, via jealousy, to madness: "Make the Moor thank me, love me, and reward me, / For making him egregiously an ass, / And practicing upon his peace and quiet / Even to madness" (289–293).

Glossary

high-wrought flood (2) heavy sea.

molestation (16) a tumult.

designment halts (22) plan is crippled.

sufferance (23) [Archaic] suffering; disaster.

Veronesa (26) ship fitted in Verona.

paragons (62) [Obsolete] surpasses.

quirks (63) ingenuities.

enwheel (87) encompass.

birdlime (126) a kind of paste.

frieze (126) rough cloth.

white (133) a pun on "wight," [Archaic] a person.

profane . . . counsellor (164) worldly and licentious.

home (165) to the point, bluntly.

clyster pipes (177) syringes; enema tubes.

conveniences (233) compatibilities.

heave the gorge (234) become nauseated.

pregnant (238) likely, most significant.

humane seeming (241) courteous appearance.

salt (242) lecherous.

incorporate (266) carnal, or fleshly.

sudden in choler (275) quick to anger.

rank garb (310) gross manner.

Act II
Scene 2

Summary

The herald reads a proclamation declaring a night of general festivities to celebrate both the destruction of the Turkish fleet and Othello's recent marriage.

Commentary

This short scene is occasionally combined with the scene that follows. Chiefly, it functions in approximately the same way that a curtain is pulled in a modern theater to indicate the passing of time. We know that the Turkish fleet has suffered "perdition," largely due to the "noble" and "valiant" efforts of Othello, and that the rejoicing celebrates the military victory and also the general's recent marriage. In short, the Moor has proclaimed a holiday to be held from five o'clock until eleven, during which the soldiers and citizens can dance, make bonfires, or make "revels [however] his [addiction] leads him" (6).

Style & Language

Dramatically, this mood of merrymaking and celebration is a strong contrast to the tragedy that is about to follow and, in addition, the chaos gives Iago sufficient time and opportunity to set his traps for the unsuspecting Othello. Also, this feasting and dancing takes place at night, and earlier Iago proclaimed that "hell and night / Must bring this monstrous birth [of his evil design] to the world's light" (I.3, 409–410). This scene preludes that horror.

Glossary

mere perdition (3) complete destruction.

addiction (6) an inclination.

Act II
Scene 3

Summary

Cassio, commanding the night watch during the time of feasting and drinking, takes his orders from Othello, who directs the soldiers to drink with moderation and keep the peace. Cassio and Iago, his second in command, will see to this. Then Othello and Desdemona retire to bed, the first night they will spend together since their marriage.

Alone, Iago makes suggestive remarks about Desdemona to Cassio, which Cassio turns aside; then Iago invites him to drink. Cassio declines, but Iago wheedles and urges him, until Cassio finally relents. Iago spurs Roderigo into a fight with Cassio; others join in and Iago sends Roderigo to ring the alarm bell, waking Othello and bringing him and his armed men to the spot. Othello demands to know who started the fight, and feigning reluctance, Iago names Cassio. Othello relieves Cassio of his post on the spot. Then he and Desdemona return to bed.

Iago advises Cassio to ask Desdemona to speak on his behalf with her husband. Cassio agrees, and Iago uses his wife, Emilia, to arrange a private meeting between Cassio and Desdemona.

Commentary

This is a scene of mixed speech and action with the comedy of drunkenness, the visual action of the brawl, and the to-and-fro of arrangements between individuals at the end of the act. Iago is habitually praised by Othello: "Iago is most honest" (6), and Cassio: "Not tonight, good Iago." (28).

In his conversation with Cassio, Iago begins by speaking of Desdemona in a sexually suggestive manner, "she is sport for Jove" (16) and "I'll warrant her full of game" (18), which Cassio deflects. Iago then tries to ply Cassio with drink, but Cassio refuses politely and with reason: "I have very poor and unhappy brains for drinking. I could well wish courtesy would invent some other custom of entertainment" (30–32). Relying on Cassio's good manners to override his determination, Iago continues to press, and Cassio eventually gives in.

When Cassio protests with elaborate carefulness that he is not drunk, he is simultaneously a figure of comedy and dreadful anticipation: "Do not think, gentlemen, I am drunk; this is my ancient, this is my right hand, and this is my left hand. I am not drunk now, I can stand well enough, and I speak well enough" (97–99). His every word calls attention to his drunken state and his loss of good judgment.

Iago tells Montano that Cassio is a habitual drunkard and that Othello has misjudged in promoting such an unreliable person. When Cassio appears, Montano upbraids him for being drunk, and Cassio turns on him, wounding Montano with his sword. This scene is often played with much noise and running about the stage, through patches of light and dark. Any number of actors could join in, and the more chaotic it appears, the better. However, it is a serious plot development scene and cannot be played for comedy.

Othello has been roused from his marriage bed, and his anger is intense. He sees the matter immediately as one of incompetence in his subordinates. He accuses them of uncivilized behavior, doing the enemy's work by destroying the army: "For Christian shame, put by this barbarous brawl" (153), and he threatens the next person to move with execution. There are potential political consequences: if the people of Cyprus think there is a rebellion, they may rise also, so Othello orders, "Silence that dreadful bell: it frights the isle / From her propriety" (135–136). His anger will fall on the man who began the brawl, and, slipping back into his old habit of relying on his *ancient* (ensign) rather than seeking out his new lieutenant, Othello calls directly on Iago to tell him who it is. Iago replies: "I had rather have this tongue cut from my mouth / Than it should do offence to Michael Cassio" (202–203), a blatantly obvious betrayal built into a semblance of reluctance. Othello, trusting Iago, is completely taken in: "I know, Iago, Thy honesty and love doth mince this matter, making in light to Cassio" (227–229). In this scene, Iago supplants Cassio, regaining his place nearest to Othello.

Cassio, sobered, grieves for his lost reputation: "I have lost the immortal part of myself, and what remains is bestial" (242–244), and Iago replies "Reputation is an idle and most false imposition, often got without merit, and lost without deserving" (247–248). Later, in discussion with Othello, Iago will argue the opposite view. As a two-faced follower of Janus, he can advocate either side of an argument when needed to serve his own ends. Iago plays a different personality to each

companion in this scene, urging Cassio to drink up and join the celebration, standing back with Montano as an observer of unwise behavior, describing the quarrel to Othello in such a way as to show Cassio
as drunken and incompetent, and finally being the helpful friend to
Cassio, suggesting a course of action for his reinstatement.

Cassio is overwhelmed with guilt and remorse, and, eagerly accept-
ing Iago's offer of a course of action, walks straight into his trap. Iago's
soliloquy of self-justification contains a twisted echo of Cassio's "Do
not think I am drunk" speech. Whereas Cassio spoke from foolishness,
Iago speaks from malevolence: "And what's he then that says I play the
villain, when this advice is free I give, and honest?" (303–304). He has
now refined his plan and outlines the diabolical details: Cassio will plead
with Desdemona, who will plead with Othello. Iago will tell Othello
that Desdemona wants Cassio back for sexual purposes. "I'll pour this
pestilence into his ear" (323). Iago will whisper poisonous words into
Othello's ear, killing Othello from the inside by filling his mind with
unbearable jealousy.

Glossary

cast (14) dismissed.

stoup (27) a two-quart tankard.

pottle-deep (51) to the bottom of the tankard.

canakin (66) a drinking pot.

swag-bellied (75) loose-bellied.

Almain (79) a German.

lown (88) a lout or rascal.

twiggen (143) wicker-covered.

mazzard (146) [Obsolete] the head.

propriety (167) proper order.

quarter (171) friendliness.

censure (184) judgment.

unlace (185) to undo.

entreats his pause (220) begs him to stop.

imposition (260) a quality imposed by others.

discourse fustian (272) to speak nonsense.

Hydra (298) the many-headed beast killed by Hercules.

probal (333) provable by.

Act III
Scene 1

Summary

Cassio meets with a group of musicians and a clown (a countryman) whom he sends to find Emilia. Iago sends Emilia out to speak with him, and she reports that Desdemona and Othello are discussing the events of last night. Desdemona has spoken up for Cassio, and Othello, who likes him, has undertaken to bring him back into favor when the right moment comes.

Commentary

This scene serves as a kind of comic relief—that is, it gives the audience's emotions a brief pause from the tension of the preceding acts and offers the audience some respite before it is plunged into the highly emotional scenes that very swiftly follow. The setting is next morning, outside the castle, where Cassio has arranged for a group of musicians to entertain Othello and Desdemona.

In addition to the musicians, there is a clown, or jester, a figure that appears in many Renaissance plays and could be counted on to entertain the audience with his physical nimbleness and his witty double entendres. Here the clown makes humorous reference to "wind" instruments and purposely confuses "tails" and "tales" in several coarse puns before he pokes fun at the musicians' performance. Othello does not care for the music, and so the clown dismisses them with money and bids them to "vanish into the air, away!" (21).

Cassio then gives the clown a gold piece and instructs him to tell Emilia, "the gentlewoman that attends the [General's wife]" (26–27), that he (Cassio) wishes to talk with her.

Iago enters as the clown exits and notes that Cassio has not been to bed yet. Cassio confirms it; he has decided to follow Iago's suggestion and talk with Emilia and see if she can convince Desdemona to speak with him. Iago is obviously pleased and offers to keep the Moor busy so that the "converse and business" (40) of Cassio and

Desdemona "may be more free" (41). The dramatic irony here (the double meaning that the audience recognizes but that the character—in this case Cassio—does not) is that Iago will keep Othello "busy" observing his wife and his courtly ex-lieutenant exchanging serious conversation. Upon Iago's exit, Cassio remarks about him that he (Cassio) "never knew / A Florentine more kind and honest" than Iago (42–43). The irony here is obvious. The audience certainly hopes that *many* Florentines are more honest than Iago.

Emilia enters and greets the Moor's ex-lieutenant and expresses her disappointment and sorrow at his misfortunes. From her, Cassio happily learns that already Desdemona "speaks . . . stoutly" (47) to her husband in Cassio's defense, but because Cassio wounded Cyprus' governor, a man of "great fame . . . and great affinity" (48–49), Othello cannot yet reinstate Cassio as his lieutenant. Yet Desdemona thinks that there may be some hope, for Othello "protests he loves you, / And . . . [will] take the safest [soonest] occasion . . . to bring you in again" (50–53). The news is indeed good and should satisfy Cassio, but fate makes him too impatient to resume his lieutenancy. Thus Cassio beseeches Emilia to arrange for him to speak with Desdemona alone. Emilia agrees.

Glossary

quillets (24) quips; puns.

affinity (48) kinship; family.

Act III
Scene 2

Summary

Othello sends a letter back to Venice by ship and makes an inspection of the fortifications.

Commentary

The letter to Venice sent with the ship's pilot would announce that Cyprus is safe after the destruction of the Turkish fleet. While Othello inspects the works, Iago's brings Cassio to Desdemona.

Glossary

do my duties (2) voice my loyalty.

works (2) fortifications.

Act III
Scene 3

Summary

Cassio speaks to Desdemona, asking her to intercede with Othello on his behalf. Desdemona willingly agrees, knowing that Cassio is an old friend of Othello's. She promises to speak of him with her husband repeatedly until the quarrel is patched up and Cassio is recalled.

When Othello and Iago enter, Cassio, who is embarrassed because of his antics the previous night, embraces Desdemona and departs. Iago seizes the opportunity to make an undermining comment—"Ha, I like not that"—that rankles in Othello's mind. Desdemona speaks of Cassio, and Othello, to please her, agrees to see him, but he is distracted by his private thoughts.

In a conversation with Iago, in which Iago continues to imply that he knows something that he refuses to divulge, Othello denies that he would give himself over to jealousy. In his denial, he shows himself most vulnerable. He is consumed with doubt and suspicion. Othello voices his old fears that Brabantio was right, that it was unnatural for Desdemona to love him, that he was too horrible to be loved, and that it could not last. Iago leaves, and Othello contemplates his situation: He could be tricked, married to a woman who is already looking at other men, and he fears that he must wipe her out of his heart. He tries to tell himself that it is not true.

When Desdemona re-enters, Othello's aspect is changed; he watches her intently, looking for signs, and brushes away her handkerchief when she seeks to sooth him. They go in to dinner, and Emilia picks up the fallen handkerchief, one that her husband, Iago, often urged her to steal from Desdemona. Emilia decides to have a copy made to give to Iago, but he enters, sees the handkerchief, and snatches it from her.

When Othello enters, Iago sees that Othello cannot regain his peace of mind. His speech is fevered, sweeping and frantic; he believes that his wife has been unfaithful to him. Othello then turns on Iago with savage intensity and demands to see the proof of Desdemona's infidelity. Cornered, Iago produces the dream story: Cassio spoke in his sleep, embraced him, called him Desdemona, and cursed the Moor. Iago tells Othello that he has seen Cassio wipe his brow with a handkerchief embroidered with strawberries; Othello recognizes this handkerchief as the one he gave to Desdemona.

Othello dismisses love and calls for vengeance. Certainty has freed his mind from doubt and confusion. Now he swears action, and Iago swears to help him. Othello wants Cassio dead, Iago agrees to do it, and then Othello wonders how to kill Desdemona.

Commentary

This scene, often called the "temptation scene," is the most important scene in the entire play and one of the most well-known scenes in all drama. In it, Iago speaks carefully and at length with Othello and plants the seeds of suspicion and jealousy which eventually bring about the tragic events of the play. Ironically, it is Desdemona's innocent attempt to reconcile Othello with Cassio that gives Iago the opportunity to wreak vengeance upon Othello, thereby causing the murder and suicide that bring this tragedy to its violent conclusion.

Literary Device

Ironically also, when the curtains for this act part, they reveal the loveliest scene in the entire play: the garden of the Cyprian castle. Desdemona, the well-meaning bride, has been talking with Cassio and tells him that she is sure that she can influence her husband in Cassio's behalf. Emilia is present and adds her own good wishes for Cassio; she too hopes that Desdemona will be successful. But when Emilia adds that her husband, Iago, grieves "as if the cause [for Cassio's demotion] were his" (4) and that his friendship with the Moor has been severed, even the most casual listener in the audience would probably gasp in disbelief. Emilia's comment is followed by another comment that is equally startling: Desdemona, speaking of Iago, says, "O, that's an honest fellow" (5). The dramatic irony is especially keen here as Desdemona tells Cassio that she is convinced that she "will have [her] lord and [him] again / As friendly as [they] were" (6–7).

Literary Device

Cassio expresses his gratitude, but he urges Desdemona not to delay, for if Othello waits too long to appoint a new lieutenant, he may "forget my love and service" (18). Again, Desdemona is most reassuring, stating that it is not in her character to violate a vow of friendship. (Later, Othello will believe not only that she has violated a vow of friendship, but that she has violated their vows of marriage.)

Desdemona jests to Cassio that she will "talk him [Othello] out of patience; / His bed shall seem a school . . . I'll intermingle everything he does / With Cassio's suit" (23–26). (This too is ironically ominous; within an hour, Othello's notion of his marriage bed will be filled with false visions of Cassio.) Desdemona's final lines here are prophetic: As Cassio's solicitor, she would "rather die / Than give [his] cause away" (27–28).

Emilia then notes that Othello and Iago are approaching. When the Moor and Iago enter, Cassio excuses himself hurriedly, saying that he is too ill at ease to speak with the general at this time. And it is at this point that Iago, who is ready to make the most of every incident and occasion, begins to taint Othello's belief in Desdemona's fidelity.

Character Insight

Iago represents himself as an honest, but reluctant, witness. His "Ha! I like not that!" (35) is a blatant lie; this fraudulent tsk-tsking hides Iago's true delight; nothing could satisfy his perversity more. But because Othello sees nothing amiss, Iago must make a show of not wanting to speak of it, or of Cassio, while all the time insinuating that Cassio was not just leaving, but that he was "steal[ing] away so guilty-like" (39). Iago's words here are filled with forceful innuendo, and as he pretends to be a man who cannot believe what he sees, he reintroduces jealousy into Othello's subconscious.

Desdemona greets her husband and, without guilt, introduces Cassio's name into their conversation. Here, fate plays a major role in this tragedy; not even Iago wholly arranged this swift, coincidental confrontation of Othello, Desdemona, and Cassio, and certainly the pathos of Desdemona's position here is largely due to no other factor than fate. Desdemona could not purposely have chosen a worse time to mention Cassio's name to her husband. In addition, she innocently refers to Cassio as a "suitor." All these coincidences will fester later in Othello's subconscious as Iago continues to fire the Moor's jealousy. But for now, Othello is without suspicion, even as his wife speaks openly of Cassio's wish to be reinstated as his lieutenant and of her own wish for their reconciliation. She sees no villainy in Cassio's face, she says; Cassio "errs in ignorance and not in cunning" (49). As another example of dramatic irony, note how clearly the audience can see the contrast between Cassio and Iago, a man who certainly errs—at least morally—in his own "cunning." The characters in the play, however, with the exception of Iago, are blind to Iago's duplicitous nature.

Othello seems to be concerned with other matters. Obviously, he will do what his wife asks, but his thoughts are on other things. He does not wish to call Cassio back at the moment, but Desdemona is insistent. Perhaps she is merely young and eager to have her requests granted, or perhaps she is too eager to prove to herself that her new husband is obedient; whatever the reason, she harries Othello about *when* he will reinstate Cassio as his lieutenant: " . . . to-night at supper? . . . / To-morrow dinner then? . . . / to-morrow night; on Tuesday morn; / On Tuesday noon, or night; on Wednesday morn. / I prithee, name the time, but let it not / Exceed three days . . . . When shall he come? / Tell me, Othello" (57–68). Even though she did promise Cassio not to delay speaking to Othello about the matter, such annoying insistence seems unnecessary, and it leads to Othello's becoming mildly vexed with his wife's childish pestering: "Prithee, no more; let him come when he will, / I will deny thee nothing" (74–75).

Desdemona realizes that Othello's answer is curt, and she emphasizes that this is an important matter and not a trifle that she is asking. To this, Othello stresses again that he will deny her nothing, but, in return, he asks for a bit of time so that he can be alone; he will join her shortly.

Literary Device

As Desdemona leaves, Othello chides himself for being irritated by his wife. Lovingly he sighs, "Excellent wretch! Perdition catch my soul, / But I do love thee! and when I love thee not, / Chaos is come again" (90–92). There is an element of prophecy here not only in Desdemona's and Othello's farewells to one another, but also in their lines and in the remainder of the Moor's first speech after Desdemona leaves. In a metaphorical sense, perdition will soon catch Othello's soul, and chaos will soon replace order in his life.

When Iago is alone with Othello, he resumes his attack on his general's soul. Out of seemingly idle curiosity, he asks if Desdemona was correct when she referred to the days when Othello was courting her; did Cassio indeed "know of your love?" (95). Here he prods Othello's memory to recall that Desdemona and Cassio have known each other for some time. Then again playing the reluctant confidant, he begs, as it were, not to be pressed about certain of his dark thoughts. One can see how skillfully Iago makes use of his public reputation for honesty.

It is necessary to remember throughout the play and especially in this scene that Iago has a reputation for complete honesty. It is for this reason that Othello is alarmed by Iago's hesitations and "pursed brow";

Othello knows that Iago is not a "false disloyal knave" (121) and that he is "full of love and honesty" (118). If Iago fears something, it must be a concern "working from the heart" (123). Othello is convinced that Iago is withholding something and asks for his ruminations, the "worst of thoughts / The worst of words" (132–133). What Iago is doing, of course, is making Othello believe that Iago's honor is at stake if he confesses his fears. Thus he lies to Othello again, saying that he is unwilling to speak further because he may be "vicious in [his] guess" (145).

One should never doubt that Iago *will* speak the "worst of thoughts" (132), although at first he does not answer directly. First, he speaks only the word "jealousy" aloud, fixing it in Othello's imagination; then, sanctimoniously, he warns his general against this evil, this "green ey'd monster" (166), and refers to the "wisdom" of Othello, implying that the general is not one to be trapped by his emotions. Filled with what appears to be moral fervor, Iago then proceeds to a glorification of *reputation*. One might profitably recall Iago's antithetical views on the same subject when he was talking with Cassio earlier. In Act II, Scene 3, Iago told Cassio that "reputation is an idle and most false imposition; oft got without merit, and lost without deserving" (268–270). Here, Iago seemingly holds reputation in the highest esteem; it is the "jewel of [a man's] soul" ("who steals my purse steals trash . . . / But he that filches from me my good name / Robs me of that which not enriches him, / And makes me poor indeed") (156–161).

Othello hears, and his "O misery!" (171) tells us that already he has begun to suffer aching pangs of jealousy, even though he has vowed not to be of a jealous nature. He swears that he will "see before I doubt; when I doubt, prove" (190). And Iago approves of such a stance; he, of course, is in a position to let human nature run its course and "prove" what it wishes—irrationally. He knows that man, being human, is flawed and subject to fears and irrational suspicions. He then asks the Moor to use his "free and noble nature" (199) to determine for himself the truth of the behavior between Desdemona and Cassio. But he reminds Othello that Desdemona is a Venetian lady and "in Venice they [wives] do not let [even God] see the pranks / They dare not show their husbands" (202–203). In other words, the faithless wife is a well-known member of Venetian society.

Here the reader should recall Othello's words to the Duke of Venice; he confessed that he knew very little of the world except for that pertaining to warfare. Othello is a master of games on the battlefield, but he is innocent of social games. Iago also urges Othello to recall that

Desdemona deceived her own father by marrying Othello. To Brabantio, Desdemona pretended to be afraid of Othello's dark looks; she pretended to shake and tremble at Othello's exotic demeanor, yet "she lov'd
them [Othello's features] most" (207). The implication is clear; Iago
does not have to state it: If Desdemona deceived her own flesh and
blood, she might just as naturally deceive her husband.

The logic of these lines is forceful, and Iago is astute enough to pause
now and then, begging his superior's forgiveness, and, at the same time,
attributing his own frankness to his devotion and regard for Othello.
When we hear the Moor say, "I am bound to thee for ever" (213), we
feel that indeed he has been irrevocably trapped.

Before the two men part, Iago goes to further pains to make Othello believe in his honesty and also to insure that Othello's jealousy has
been sufficiently inflamed. He must also measure how well he has suc-
ceeded thus far. Iago stresses that Cassio is his "worthy friend"; in other
words, one does not lie about one's friends and, therefore, the Moor
must not exaggerate in his imagination what he hears. Yet Iago is certain that Othello has already exaggerated to himself everything he has
just heard. For that reason, Iago's remark to Othello that all this has "a
little dash'd your spirits" (214) is a gross understatement. Othello is no
longer as sure as he was of Desdemona's fidelity, for he ponders on the
possibility of " . . . nature erring from itself—" (227). This thought is
similar to his father-in-law's observation in Act I, Scene 2, when Brabantio spoke of "nature erring"—when Desdemona "unnaturally" chose
Othello, a man not of her own race or culture. Othello turns and asks
that Iago's wife, Emilia, watch Desdemona closely. Then he bids Iago
farewell, painfully asking himself why he married at all; it is obvious to
him that "this honest creature [Iago] doubtless / Sees and knows more,
much more, than he unfolds" (242–243).

Now we hear Othello in a soliloquy (258–277), and the range of
the imagery he uses underscores the appalling change in his character.
There is only one thing now of which Othello is certain—the "exceed-
ing honesty" of Iago. The Moor is obsessed with the need to prove or
disprove Desdemona's fidelity. If he indeed finds her false, he'll "whis-
tle her off and let her down the wind / To prey at fortune"
(262–263)—that is, he will turn her out and make her shift for herself. And here he begins to look for reasons for her unfaithfulness. Con-
vulsed with introspection, he curses his black skin and his lack of social
graces and also the fact that he is "into the vale of years" (266) (he is

much older than Desdemona)—all these things, he fears, could turn a woman from her husband's bed.

Othello's mental agony approaches the emotional climax of the play; here is the first turning point of the drama. Othello's mind and soul are torn with irrational images of Desdemona's infidelity and of his own unworthiness. Othello sees himself as an old man, an old cuckold, one who has treasured Desdemona blindly, beyond reason. Hours ago, he was filled with the spirit of a young bridegroom; now he is reduced to ignominy. Once he felt he was one of the "great ones" (273); now his pride in himself and in Desdemona's love for him is destroyed. Othello is ravaged by self-loathing, reduced to comparing himself to a dungeoned toad; he is cursed by a "destiny unshunnable" (275).

And yet, as Desdemona and Emilia enter, he is able to move from this state of abject hopelessness to a momentary appeal to heaven (278) when he declares that he will *not* believe that his wife is false to him. In his few words with Desdemona, he speaks faintly, pleading that he has a headache. When Desdemona offers to bind his aching head with her handkerchief, he declines because the handkerchief is too small. He pushes it from him and it falls unnoticed to the floor. This dropped, unnoticed handkerchief should not escape our notice. Desdemona carries it because she treasures it deeply. It was one of her first gifts from Othello, and he has asked her to keep it with her always, and she has; in fact, Emilia has seen Desdemona, on occasion, kiss the handkerchief and talk to it. Later, this handkerchief in Cassio's possession will be sufficient "proof" for Othello to abandon all faith in Desdemona.

Style & Language

Alone, Emilia picks up the handkerchief. She knows how deeply Desdemona treasures it, but she recalls that Iago has asked her many times to "steal" it. She is puzzled by his request, but now she has an opportunity to have the embroidery pattern copied, and she can give it to her whimsical husband. Here it is significant that twice Emilia uses the verb *steal* and also the verb *filch* when she refers to Iago's request (lines 293, 309, and 315).

Iago enters and, after a brief exchange with his wife, learns that she has the very handkerchief that he has longed for. He snatches it from her and refuses to tell her why he wants it. After Emilia leaves, he reveals the next step in his plan: he will go to Cassio's lodgings, leave the handkerchief there, and let Cassio find it. Cassio will keep it and then Othello will see it in the ex-lieutenant's possession. By this time, Othello's suspicions will be ripe with Iago's "poison" (325), for "trifles light as air

/ Are to the jealous confirmations strong / As proofs of holy writ" (322–324). Othello will then conclude that Desdemona either gave the handkerchief to Cassio as a token of their love or left it at Cassio's lodgings after a rendezvous. In fact, a conclusion is hardly necessary; for a mind as inflamed with jealousy as Othello's, the handkerchief itself is metaphor enough. Even now Othello's blood "burn[s] like the mines of sulphur" (329). This suggestion of hellfire by Iago is a reflection of his own diabolical role in this villainy.

When Othello enters, it is evident to Iago, and to us, that he is a fallen man. Never more shall he find repose. Neither the opium of poppies nor the distillation of the mandrake root will help him find sleep. Momentarily, Othello seems to revive his senses, snarling at Iago's villainy and sending him away, then he slumps into despair. Iago's evil has "set [the Moor] on the rack" (335), and Othello wishes in vain that he had remained blind to his wife's *alleged* infidelity. In his imagination, he has seen "her stol'n hours of lust . . . [and tasted] Cassio's kisses on her lips" (338–341). He would have been happier, he cries, if his entire company of soldiers had "tasted her sweet body" (346) and he had remained ignorant of the entire episode. But now this mental torment of suspicion gnaws at him until he knows no peace.

The superb "farewell speech" that follows emphasizes how much Othello has lost—he, the model commander, the premier soldier—his "occupation's gone!" (357). Iago appears incredulous, and it is then that Othello turns on him with words that make Iago only too aware of the danger that faces him. At last Othello utters a true appraisal of Iago: "villain, be sure thou prove my love a whore" (359). But schemer that Iago is, he knows what must be done to protect himself; he must feign another vow of honesty and concern for Othello's welfare. The Moor, he says, has taught him a valuable lesson. "I'll love no friend, sith love breeds such offence" (380). Othello promptly concedes that Iago *is* honest, and the villain knows that for the time being he is safe. He turns to his general and fawns over his master's distress, noting that Othello is "eaten up with passion" (391).

In unusually coarse imagery, Iago then introduces the subject of what kind of evidence would resolve Othello's doubts. The bestial images that Iago conjures up reek of base sexuality, for now Iago no longer needs to rely on innuendo. Now he tells Othello a bold lie, claiming that he himself slept beside Cassio recently; kept awake by a raging toothache that night, Iago says that Cassio moaned in his sleep for "Sweet Desdemona" (419) and cautioned her to hide their love.

Then Cassio seized Iago's hand, kissed him hard on the mouth, and threw his leg over Iago's thigh, kissing him all the while, and cursing fate, which "gave [Desdemona] to the Moor!" (421–26). This is Iago's "proof" that makes it perfectly clear to him that Cassio has had illicit relations with Desdemona.

Othello is beside himself. "O monstrous! monstrous!" (427) he cries. But again the ingenious Iago is quick to remind his master that, in reality, this was no more than Cassio's *dream*. Othello, however, thinks otherwise—as Iago was certain he would. In his rage, the Moor declares that he will tear Desdemona to pieces. Here, compare this madman, incensed by Iago's poison, with the noble Moor who, only a few hours ago, repeatedly demonstrated such complete command of himself.

Yet Iago must be sure that Othello is sufficiently mad; therefore, he makes reference to Desdemona's handkerchief with its intricate strawberry embroidery; Othello immediately remembers it as the very one he gave to his wife. Iago tells the Moor that only today he saw Cassio "wipe his beard" (439) with it. Othello is enraged to the point where he is convinced that absolutely all of his suspicions are true. "All my fond love thus do I blow to heaven. / 'Tis gone," he exclaims (445–446), and in highly rhetorical lines, he dwells upon "black vengeance" and "tyrannous hate" (446–449).

Iago urges Othello to be patient, arguing that he may change his mind, and there follows the well-known Pontic Sea (i.e., the Black Sea) simile, in which Othello compares his "bloody thoughts" (447) to the sea's compulsive current, one which never ebbs but keeps on its course until it reaches its destination, the junction of the Propontic and the Hellespont (453–460). In this simile, Othello stresses his high status (as we might expect a tragic hero to do), identifying himself with large and mighty elements of nature. Equally important, this simile makes clear the absoluteness in Othello's character; once he has decided which course to take, he cannot turn back, and this decision does much to make plausible the almost incredible actions that follow.

Othello solemnly vows to execute "a capable and wide revenge" (459), and then he kneels. He uses such words as *heaven, reverence,* and *sacred,* and it is as though he sees himself as a rightful scourge of evil, as executing *public* justice and not merely doing *personal* revenge. Iago bids the Moor not to rise yet, and he himself kneels and dedicates himself to "wrong'd Othello's service" (467). Then as both rise, Othello "greets" Iago's love and delegates a test of Iago's loyalty: See to it that

Cassio is dead within three days. One cannot imagine more welcome words to Iago. As for Desdemona's fate, Othello says that he will withdraw and find "some swift means of death" (447). Othello's soul is so hopelessly ensnared in Iago's web of treachery that he proclaims Iago as his new lieutenant and states tragically, "I am your own for ever" (449).

By the end of Act III, Scene 3, Iago has secured a shaky dominance over Othello. He is within reach of his original objective of driving Othello to despair, but his victory is not secure, as Othello may yet think to blame Iago again for his suffering and turn against him. While Cassio and Desdemona live, Iago has gained only a little time in which to secure his position.

Glossary

shrift (24) [Archaic] a confessional.

mamm'ring (70) hesitating.

poise (82) weight; grave importance.

conceit (115) a thought or fancy.

leet and law days (140) meetings of the court.

fineless (173) unlimited.

seel (210) to close.

vile success (222) evil consequences.

happily (238) [Archaic] haply, by chance.

hold her free (255) believe her to be guiltless.

haggard (255) a wild hawk.

jesses (261) straps for holding a hawk to the trainer's wrist.

napkin (287) a handkerchief.

mandragora (330) a soporific, or substance causing sleep.

Pioners (346) manual laborers doing the least desirable kinds of work.

mortal engines (355) deadly artillery.

bolster (399) lie together.

prime (403) lustful.

Act III
Scene 4

Summary

Desdemona sends for Cassio to tell him that she has spoken with Othello; she is also worried that she has lost her handkerchief. When Othello enters, he claims a headache and asks her for a handkerchief to bind his head, but he will have only the embroidered strawberry handkerchief. In vain, Desdemona tries to deflect his questions about the handkerchief, speaking again of Cassio. Othello walks out in fury.

Cassio gives Bianca Desdemona's handkerchief, which he found in his lodgings (Iago had placed it there) and asks her to make a copy of it for him, as he will have to return the original when he finds the owner. Bianca immediately recognizes it as belonging to a woman and berates Cassio for having another mistress.

Commentary

Coming after the emotional intensity of the previous scene, this scene looks at some of the same themes from different viewpoints. In particular, it takes a more roundabout look at jealousy.

The Clown provides some contrasting comic relief, taking words only at face value, and this little diversion covers the plot move where Desdemona sends for Cassio. Desdemona has an underlying worry, the loss of the handkerchief, but Emilia, who does know what happened, does not tell her. Desdemona is confident, or at least hopeful, that her husband is not jealous, while Emilia suspects that all men are jealous.

The interview between Othello and Desdemona begins stiffly and formally: "Well, my good lady" (30), and she, taking her cue from him, answers formally. They speak at cross-purposes, Othello claiming her moist hand indicates lust, she suggesting it means youth and innocence, and while making a speech on her need to curb her inclinations, the old happy love suddenly hits him again, and he acknowledges: "'tis a good hand, A frank one." (39). The bond between them is reestablished, and he calls her by a pet name, chuck. But the bond breaks when she mentions Cassio. Othello demands her handkerchief, which she cannot produce.

Othello tells the story of the handkerchief: it is an heirloom in his family, given by an Egyptian witch to his mother as a charm to keep her husband's love. If the handkerchief were lost, the love would go. This confection of far-fetched story elements seems to be believed implicitly by both Othello and Desdemona, who, under stress, ascribe wider powers and cosmic meaning to a handkerchief that, up until now, was simply a personal love token.

Literary Device

Desdemona is panicked into lying: "It is not lost, but what an if it were?" (82) and tries to lead the conversation back to Cassio. Othello has caught her out. He repeats "the handkerchief" over her words, working himself up into a fury, and storms off. All he has established is that she does not have it, but just the thought of the handkerchief is enough to madden him, torturing him now with the mental picture of Cassio wiping himself with it. The handkerchief, which once symbolized love and loyalty, now means betrayal.

Style & Language

Iago brings Cassio to Desdemona, and they discuss Othello's anger. Emilia speaks of irrational jealousy: "But jealous souls will not be answer'd so; / They are not ever jealous for the cause, / But jealous for they are jealous: @'tis a monster, begot upon itself, born on itself." (157–160). These lines echo Iago's "It is the green ey'd monster which doth mock that meat it feeds on" (III.3, 170–171), hinting that Iago and Emilia have talked or argued about jealousy in their own married life. Meanwhile Cassio and Bianca argue over a handkerchief Cassio found in his lodgings. Bianca, recognizing a woman's handkerchief, jealously suspects that Cassio has a new love.

Desdemona's straightforward trust contrasts with Othello's sulky suspicion. Emilia's view of jealousy as a natural characteristic of irrational men contrasts with Othello's real personal sufferings of the previous scene. Desdemona and Emilia discuss possible reasons for Othello's bad mood and suspend judgment for lack of sure evidence. This contrasts with Othello's train of thought in the previous act, where, with less actual evidence before him, he changed his whole view of himself and his marriage.

The dramatic irony is that the most jealous indignation is expressed over offenses that did not happen: Othello jealous about his wife; Bianca jealous about Cassio; Iago formerly jealous about Emilia. Each character attempts to cope as an individual, except Emilia, who has a theory that jealousy is a constituent part of masculinity. The evidence before her own eyes backs up her assessment.

Glossary

crusadoes (27) Portuguese gold coins.

heraldry (48) heraldic symbolism.

Egyptian (57) a Gypsy.

mummy (75) fluid drained from embalmed bodies.

blank (129) a target; bull's-eye.

unhatched practice (142) a budding plot.

puddled (144) muddied.

unhandsome warrior (152) unskilled soldier.

toy (157) a fancy or a trifle.

dial (176) a full twelve hours on the face of a clock.

continuate (179) uninterrupted.

Act IV
Scene 1

Summary

In a conversation with Othello, Iago says that Cassio has confessed to sex with Desdemona. This revelation is too much for Othello, who becomes incoherent and faints. When Cassio enters, Iago claims that Othello has epilepsy and has had seizures before. Rather than revive him, they must let the fit take its course. Iago sends Cassio away, telling him to come back later. Othello, regaining consciousness, talks of himself as one among many cuckolds, but Iago tells him to hide and observe Cassio, who is returning. Iago says he will draw Cassio out to tell of his amorous adventures with Desdemona.

Othello withdraws, too emotionally involved to understand that Iago is manipulating him, and Iago talks with Cassio about Bianca. Othello sees his smiles and laughter but cannot hear the details and believes he is joking about how much Desdemona loves him. Then Bianca herself enters, with Desdemona's handkerchief, which she throws back at Cassio. Seeing his wife's handkerchief in the hands of Cassio's mistress is, for Othello, the "ocular proof" he sought. He is now convinced of Desdemona's infidelity and knows he must kill both Cassio and Desdemona that very night.

Commentary

Iago, while pretending to reassure Othello, is rubbing salt into his wounds. Their conversation is of hypothetical acts, whether they constitute betrayal or not, but Othello imagines them all being acted out by Desdemona and Cassio. But this is just the warm-up to the topic that Iago has discovered can most easily rouse Othello's passions: the handkerchief. Othello, in his thinking, assumes it is a symbol for his wife's honor, but Iago plays at thinking it is only a handkerchief: "being hers, she may, I think, bestow't on any man" (13). He repeats again the word "handkerchief," and Othello cries out.

Iago can see that Othello is at the edge of madness, and there is no way he can judge just how far to push him, considering his unexpectedly violent previous reaction. However, Iago cannot afford to leave Othello in his present frame of mind, where he might do something unpredictable. Therefore, he proceeds to tell Othello the direct lie: that Cassio has confessed to a sexual affair with Desdemona. Iago uses again the successful technique of hesitation, forcing Othello himself to say what Iago would have him think. Iago, the liar, comes back to the word "lie" when telling his untruth so that the word "lie" echoes with double meaning through their conversation, lacerating Othello with thoughts of two illicit lovers and, at the same time, accusing Iago for his abuse of the truth.

Othello is now raving; his words come in an anxious jumble around "handkerchief," and "confess" until he falls down in a faint. The overstressed mind seeks refuge in unconsciousness. Instead of pity or alarm, Iago only expresses satisfaction that his medicine (poison words) is working.

Cassio suggests rubbing Othello about the temples, but Iago calmly waits for him to regain consciousness and takes the opportunity to tell Cassio that Othello has epileptic seizures and bouts of madness. Such a story is Iago's insurance, in case Othello should later say something that Cassio finds strange.

Iago urges Othello to hide and watch him talk with Cassio. Othello, who had led armies into battle, is now reduced to crouching behind something, listening to a conversation he cannot well hear, and imagining Cassio and his wife laughing at him. Iago takes a great risk with this maneuver, as he has no way of controlling completely what Cassio might say or how much Othello actually overhears. He leads Cassio to laugh and joke about Bianca, trusting that Othello's mind will turn what he sees into evidence. Then, by chance, Bianca walks in with the strawberry-spotted handkerchief and berates Cassio for asking her to copy the token of his new love. Othello recognizes the handkerchief, and all other considerations are forgotten.

Othello goes directly to the point: "How shall I murder him, Iago?" Othello swears also to kill his wife this night, he curses her and weeps over her at the same time, mingling love and murder: "for she shall not live; no, my heart is turned to stone . . . " (178–179).

This is the second time Othello has sworn to kill both Cassio and Desdemona, but his continuity of love beside revenge unnerves Iago, who needs to push Othello to a definite unalloyed commitment to murder. Therefore, Iago prompts Othello to consider his personal honour: "If you be so fond over her iniquity, give her patent to offend, for if it touches not you, it comes near nobody" (199–201). The idea of giving his wife permission to take lovers so enrages Othello that he cries, "I will chop her into messes" (202), surely the most savage of all his threats, and one he later regrets.

Still Othello knows the pull of love and asks for poison so that he might kill her at a distance, but he sees justice in Iago's idea of strangling her in her bed, imagining that she has dishonored that bed. Again the agreement is made: Iago is to kill Cassio, and Othello is to kill Desdemona. Iago has profited from good luck and good organization to achieve almost complete power over Othello.

Lodovico, Desdemona's cousin, has just arrived from Venice with a letter for Othello. Expecting to see a happy newly married couple, Lodovico finds they can hardly speak to each other. When Othello strikes his wife, calling her "Devil" (235), Lodovico is shocked, but whatever he might say would only make things worse. Othello and Desdemona are involved in a personal matter to the exclusion of others, and Othello is fraught by a matter of internal conflict that excludes his wife. From the outside, it all looks like madness. Lodovico is amazed at the change in "the noble Moor . . . whose solid virtue / The shot of accident, nor dart of chance, could neither graze, nor pierce" (260–264).

Iago knows that Othello has been ordered back to Venice and Cassio has been made commander in Cyprus, so he knows the murders must be done immediately, or he will be found out. He hints to Lodovico that Othello should be watched, increasing Lodovico's suspicion that Othello is going mad.

Glossary

infected (21) stricken with the plague.

convinced or supplied (28) overcame or gratified.

A horned man's (63) a cuckold's.

ecstasy (80) a trance.

encave (82) hide.

spleen (89) anger.

unbookish (102) uninformed.

caitiff (109) a wretch.

customer (120) here, a prostitute.

hales (140) tugs at; hauls.

fitchew (146) a polecat (meaning "a whore").

hobby-horse (156) a prostitute; harlot.

undertaker (156) a person who undertakes to do something.

crocodile (247) a reference to the false tears supposedly shed by crocodiles.

Act IV
Scene 2

Summary

Othello questions Emilia about Desdemona, but she assures him that nothing immodest has taken place between her mistress and Cassio. Othello, rather than abandon his suspicions, believes Desdemona is so cunning that she has managed to deceive even her maid. Othello speaks with Desdemona in private, threatening to banish her and calling her "whore" and "strumpet"—charges that she immediately denies.

Emilia comes in, and Othello leaves. Exhausted, Desdemona knows that she is being punished, but she does not know what for. Emilia suspects that some villain has turned Othello against his wife and stirred up his jealousy. When Desdemona asks Iago's advice, he says that it is only the business of the state that makes Othello angry.

Later, in a conversation with Iago, Roderigo confesses that he has had enough of his romantic quest and plans to withdraw. Iago makes a bold move, linking his two plots together: He urges Roderigo to kill Cassio, explaining that Cassio's death will prevent Othello being sent elsewhere and, therefore, keep Desdemona in Cyprus. Roderigo allows himself to be persuaded.

Commentary

Othello is now reduced to questioning his wife's maid, Emilia, looking for evidence of Desdemona's infidelity. He has already judged and condemned her, but he is still hunting evidence, seeking to justify to himself the stand he has already taken. This is not a satisfactory frame of mind for an investigator, and it is certainly not an acceptable frame of mind for a military commander responsible for law and order in a colony. To a certain extent, Othello is indeed mad, so wrapped up in his obsession that he can hardly consider other things.

Emilia assures Othello that Desdemona is faithful and adds her own opinion: She speaks for the first time her theory that some villain is telling Othello lies to turn him against Desdemona. From now on, she develops this theory every time she thinks about it. Although she is completely correct, Emilia does not identify the "wretch" until too late. In some ways, she really believes her husband is an honest man, although her opinion of men in general is not high. Othello, instead of reconsidering his accusations, is even more bitter about Desdemona, judging her to be so deceptive that she can sin and pray and convince everyone, even her maid, of her innocence. He holds tightly to the idea that she has betrayed him, because by now he has built this idea into his view of himself.

In Othello's interview alone with Desdemona, Shakespeare balances hope and dread, ensuring emotional involvement. Desdemona declares she is his "true and loyal wife" (35) and drags out of him the accusations that she is "false as hell" (40), a "whore" (74), and a "public commoner" (75), that is, prostitute. These accusations are exaggerated, even for Othello, since he believes she has had an affair with Cassio, but in his fevered mind, and in that of many of Shakespeare's characters, there is no difference between an occasional adulterer and a full-time street prostitute. They all come under the heading of "false" women.

Desdemona immediately and completely denies the accusation, and her husband speaks scornfully and bitterly, throws money at her, as if she were a prostitute, and goes out. Having made the accusation and been denied, he reacts with anger rather than reassessment.

Desdemona's reaction to the confrontation is the opposite. She tells Emilia she is "half asleep," either as a convenient lie to keep her privacy or as an expression of emotional exhaustion. Emilia invites conversation, but her mistress, near to weeping but unable to do it, can only think of one course of action, the wedding sheets. Wedding sheets are one of the major items in a well brought-up young woman's set of household linen that she brings to her marriage. These sheets would be of the finest cloth, hand-embroidered by the bride herself, and would have taken a considerable time to make. In some Mediterranean cultures, after the marriage ceremony, the couple retire to the bedroom and consummate the marriage. The wedding sheets are then hung out on the balcony, to show to all that the bride had been a virgin. So wedding sheets have both intimate and public connotations of things being done according to correct procedure. By putting the wedding sheets on the bed, Desdemona is symbolically trying to renew and strengthen the marriage and remind Othello that he too has duties of love.

Iago is keen to hear how Othello has spoken to Desdemona but is disconcerted when she starts to weep: "Do not weep, do not weep: alas the day!" (126). Perhaps, like many men, he construes a weeping woman as a potential emotional manipulator, and Iago instinctively guards himself against any pull toward pity or mercy. He knows that she will soon be murdered by her husband, and this grief, which she suffers and weeps over now, is small trouble in comparison. In response to an abusive husband, he suggests: "Beshrew him for it!" (130), that is, nag him.

Emilia is developing her theory about the person who is corrupting Othello's mind. She calls him "some eternal villain, / Some busy and insinuating rogue, / Some cogging, cozening slave" (132–134), and Iago must stand and hear himself described in these uncomplimentary terms. In vain, Iago tries to keep her quiet.

Roderigo appears, demanding Iago's attention for a previous scheme that suddenly threatens to unwind. Roderigo regrets the situation that he has gotten himself in, and he wishes to withdraw. However, he wants to get back his jewels that he had given to Iago for Desdemona (an unsuccessful courtship gift was traditionally returned to the suitor). Iago, who has pocketed Roderigo's money and jewels for himself, must now move quickly to protect his acquisitions and to prevent Roderigo speaking directly to Desdemona and revealing Iago's illegitimate activities. Iago repeatedly replies "very well," which finally inflames the heretofore excessively patient Roderigo to an outburst of petulant rebellion: " . . . 'tis not very well. Nay, I think it is very scurvy, and begin to find myself fopp'd in it" (191–193). This perception of Roderigo's that he may have been taken for a fool is the understatement of the play.

For the audience at this point, there is the madly delightful prospect that Iago could be brought down by Roderigo, his own dupe. However, Iago joins his two plots, enrolling Roderigo in the plan to kill Cassio, and Roderigo's rebellion fades away. The quick flash of emotion in this exchange provides a variation and therefore a relief from the steadily mounting tension of Othello's thoughts and action.

Glossary

being . . . heaven (36) looking like an angel.

shambles (66) a slaughterhouse.

winks (66) shuts her eyes.

go by water (104) be rendered by tears.

small'st opinion (109) least suspicion.

callet (121) a whore, or prostitute.

cogging, cozening (132) lying, cheating.

votarist (188) a nun.

fopped (194) duped; deceived.

Act IV
Scene 3

Summary

After the supper, Othello orders Desdemona to go to bed and to dismiss her attendant. Desdemona and Emilia discuss the situation; Emilia sees the marriage with Othello as a mistake, but Desdemona regrets nothing. She has a premonition of death and requests Emilia, if she should die, to wrap her body in one of her wedding sheets, which are now on the bed. Desdemona sings the "Willow Song," remembering the maid Barbary whose lover went mad and abandoned her, and she died singing this song.

Commentary

Emilia knows something is seriously wrong, but Desdemona's mind is preoccupied with the problem of her husband's love. She loves him so much that she cannot tell whether his love is lost or is yet recoverable. She has a vague premonition of death and requests of Emilia, "If I do die before thee, prithee shroud me / In one of those same sheets" (24–25). Desdemona has reacted to this crisis with the passivity of despair and grief, as was the tradition for women abandoned. Othello, on the other hand, thinking he has lost Desdemona's love and fidelity, reacts with aggressive passions of accusations and violence.

Literary
Device

Desdemona tells the story of her mother's maid, Barbary, and her sad fate. "She was in love, and he she lov'd prov'd mad, / And did forsake her: she had a song of 'willow,' / An old thing 'twas, but it express'd her fortune, / And she died singing it" (27–30). Barbary is a parallel for Desdemona herself: her mother's maid is something like her mother's daughter, a girl under her mother's care and protection. This is the only time Desdemona mentions her mother, and she speaks of her in the distant past, as if she were dead. Desdemona's mother plays no part in the story of the courtship and marriage to Othello, and Desdemona speaks and acts as a woman alone, who takes full responsibility for her decisions.

Desdemona and Barbary are not only alone in their sorrow but are both associated with strangers. "Barbary," the name, means "foreigner." Desdemona married a foreigner, whom some called a barbarian, that is an uncivilized foreigner. Iago described the marriage as that between "an erring barbarian and a super-subtle Venetian"(I.3, 355–356), an opinion many Venetians would have held and that Desdemona would have been well aware of.

Literary Device

Desdemona sings the "Willow Song," and, in this indirect way, she faces the real possibility that Othello is going mad and will desert her and that she may die of a broken heart. The "Willow Song" is an old one, existing in many versions before Shakespeare incorporated it into his play. Of special interest is line 52 that echoes, as it were, Desdemona's thoughts in lines 19–20. In the song, it is the male lover who is false and the cause of the poor woman's sighing and weeping. Obviously the mood perfectly reflects that of Desdemona, whose love is so strong that she approves Othello's frowns, just as the "poor soul" (41) in the song approves her lover's "scorn" (52). Willow, also known as weeping willow, is associated in Shakespeare's plays with lost love. In Hamlet, staged three years before Othello, Ophelia drowns surrounded by willows and flowers; Gertrude describes the scene: "There is a willow grows askant a brook" (Hamlet IV.7, 166). Ophelia's love, Prince Hamlet, appeared mad and rejected her, and she lost her mind and died singing as she drowned. Ophelia and Barbary have almost the same story.

All through this scene, while Emilia tries to comfort and cheer Desdemona, she knows that her husband Iago has the handkerchief, a fact that she could have revealed to Desdemona but does not. Possibly Emilia hopes nothing more will be heard of the matter, or she thinks to protect her husband from accusation if the handkerchief subsequently turns up somewhere. Emilia had stood silently in the background (as a lady's maid should) when Othello demanded to see the handkerchief and Desdemona could not produce it (Act III, Scene 4), so she is aware that the handkerchief itself forms part of Othello's accusation. To speak now would seem too late, but to hide the information is not honest either.

Emilia and Desdemona make a clear contrast in their approach to marriage and fidelity. Desdemona is a romantic who has married for love and values loyalty absolutely. Emilia has a practical intelligence and assesses each situation to decide which is the best course of action. She thinks that a wife's infidelity is a serious matter, only to be undertaken for good solid reasons of advantage: "who would not make her husband a cuckold, to make him a monarch?" (74–75). The other reason for a wife to be unfaithful is in reaction to the husband's misbehavior or maltreatment: "But I do think it is their husbands' faults / If wives do fall" (86–87).

Emilia's speech at the end of Act IV on the faults of husbands neatly balances Iago's speech in Act II on the faults of wives. Both speeches were heard by Desdemona, who dismisses them as not relating to her and her love.

Glossary

stubbornness (20) roughness.

nightgown (34) a dressing-gown; robe.

store (84) to fill; populate.

peevish (88) silly.

galls (91) the ability to resent.

Act V
Scene 1

Summary

In the street at night, Iago directs Roderigo to ambush Cassio. When Cassio approaches, Roderigo attacks unsuccessfully and is wounded by Cassio. Iago, from behind, stabs Cassio in the leg and runs away while Cassio cries murder. Othello, hearing Cassio's cry, believes that Iago has done the job he has undertaken. Following Iago's lead, Othello must harden his heart against the charms of his wife and spill her blood in the bed where she has betrayed him.

Commentary

This scene is framed by Iago's comments on the importance of this night. Before the action starts, he tells Roderigo: "It makes us or it mars us, think of that, / And fix most firm thy resolution" (4–50). To Roderigo, Iago is saying "Be brave, kill Cassio, and you will have Desdemona." To himself, he is saying "Be brave, make sure Roderigo, Cassio, and Desdemona die, and you will have your revenge on Othello."

Roderigo is still wavering, nursing his last flicker of moral sense: "Be near at hand, I may miscarry in't" (6). The comfort of the coward is in belief that someone will protect him, but by agreeing to rely on Iago to make the decisions, Roderigo abdicates responsibility for his own actions and is led out to kill a man he doesn't hate for a cause he no longer thinks can be won.

Iago wastes no emotion on the prospect of Roderigo's death but acknowledges a certain satisfaction when he thinks of Cassio dead. There is the old fury of jealousy against Cassio who has the good opinions of every one, including Othello (until Iago's duplicity, that is). The unfairness of Cassio's happy life rankles Iago as evidenced in his first speech in Act I and continues to frustrate him now: "[I]f Cassio do remain, he has a daily beauty in his life, that makes me ugly" (18–20). Add this to the need to prevent Cassio talking with Othello, and his death will be Iago's pleasure.

Character
Insight

Sword fighting is a dangerous business, and certain conventions govern its honorable practice, but there is no honor in this ambush: Roderigo hides himself to strike Cassio; Cassio hits out in the dark in self-defense; and Iago, having promised to back up Roderigo, hunts him down and stabs him. To make an agreement to fight shoulder to shoulder with a comrade and then to step back and stab the man who relied on him is the worst thing a soldier can do. Having now betrayed a value in his profession, Iago exacerbates his infamy.

The cries of the dying men remind Othello of his resolution to kill Desdemona. Again he regrets what he knows he must do. He must force aside, with an iron will, his love for her: "forth of my heart those charms, thine eyes, are blotted, / Thy bed, lust-stain'd, shall with lust's blood be spotted" (34–35). He must close her eyes, stop her looking at him, before he can kill her. Again he stamps out love with overdone violence, conjuring up the image of killing her in her bed, but this mental picture begins to resemble the red and white strawberry-spotted handkerchief, the picture that drives him to madness. The bed in his mind is stained with lust, that is Desdemona's infidelities with Cassio, and will be spotted with "lust's blood" when he kills her in revenge. In that instant, Othello pictures himself killing her with a sword, as Iago will kill Cassio with a sword. Othello will spill her blood on the white sheets, but this time the blood is not from the passion and lust of first love, but from the passion and lust of desperate murder.

The further Iago sinks into villainy, the more Emilia's position has become equivocal. Put on the spot, she automatically backs up her husband, but the circumstances are more and more stretching her loyalty and producing an increasing tension based on her increased knowledge. Sooner or later, Emilia will tell what she knows. For all her words of scorn about husbands, Emilia automatically sides with her husband in what she must know is a scurrilous attack on another woman. She cries "fie upon thee, strumpet!" to which Bianca replies: "I am no strumpet, but of life as honest / As you, that thus abuse me" (120–123). In Bianca's eyes this is true, as all she is doing is standing by her own man, as Emilia is doing with hers.

At this point, Iago feels a certain satisfaction. Roderigo is dead, his money and jewels now securely in Iago's keeping, and no one else is aware of this. Cassio is badly wounded and believes he has been attacked by a gang of thieves. This, for Iago, is a less than perfect result, but Cassio might subsequently die of his injuries or be maimed and crippled, in which case his army career is over. But much is still left to be done before Iago can consider himself safe or triumphant. The night has yet to be accomplished. "This is the night that either makes me, or fordoes me quite" (127–128).

Glossary

quat (11) a pimple.

bobbed (16) cheated; swindled.

coat (25) a coat of mail worn under outer clothing.

minion (33) mistress; or hussy, as here used.

gastness (106) ghastliness, or terror.

fordoes (129) destroys.

Act V
Scene 2

Summary

Desdemona lies asleep in bed, and Othello enters, dreadfully calm and sure in what he must do. Desdemona wakens and calls him to bed, but he tells her to pray at once, repenting anything she needs to repent, and he will wait while she prays because he does not want to kill her soul. Suddenly, Desdemona realizes that Othello intends to kill her. She is afraid, although she knows she is not guilty. Knowing that she cannot convince him of her fidelity, Desdemona weeps and begs him to banish her rather than kill her, or let her live just a little more, but he stifles her, presumably with a pillow.

When Emilia knocks on the door, Othello draws the bed-curtain across, hiding the bed, and opens the door to hear the news. What Emilia reports is not what Othello expected. She says that Cassio has killed Roderigo. Then Desdemona's voice is heard from the bed, saying "falsely murdered" and Emilia calls for help. Desdemona says that she is innocent, denies that anyone has killed her, and dies.

Emilia and Othello confront each other. Emilia sees herself as a witness and will tell what she has seen, and Othello declares that he has killed Desdemona because of her infidelity. Emilia insists that Desdemona was faithful; Othello replies that Cassio had been with her, and Iago knew all about it. Now Emilia has the key idea. She says "my husband" over and over, while Othello pours out his heart on justice and how he loved her and how Iago is honest. Emilia curses Iago, calls him a liar, and cries murder to waken everyone.

Montano, Gratiano, Iago, and others rush into the bedchamber where Emilia is shouting, and she challenges Iago to defend himself, giving him one last chance to retrieve himself in her estimation. Iago says that Desdemona was indeed unfaithful with Cassio, but Emilia knows this is untrue. She tells how she found the handkerchief, which her husband had asked her to steal, and gave it to him. Iago stabs Emilia and runs out. As she dies, Emilia tells Othello that Desdemona loved him. Othello realizes, too late, that he had been tricked and manipulated.

Iago is caught and brought back. Othello and Cassio demand to know why he did it, but Iago refuses to explain and says he will never speak again. Othello, watching his world unravel, asks the men to remember him clearly, his good points and his bad, as "one that lov'd not wisely, but too well." Then he stabs himself, falls onto the bed, and dies.

Lodovico takes charge, giving Othello's house and property to Gratiano, his next of kin by marriage. Cassio will be commander and have the power to sentence Iago, and Lodovico will return to Venice with the sad news.

Commentary

Desdemona is asleep in her bed as Othello enters, carrying a candle. He is no longer the angry, vengeful husband. His soliloquy is quiet, and he seems to be more an agent of justice than the jealous cuckold. He speaks repeatedly of "the cause . . . the cause" (1)—that is, Desdemona's infidelity, and he even hesitates to speak aloud the name of Desdemona's crime before the "chaste stars" (2). At last, Othello assumes the posture of the tragic hero, grossly wrong in his determination, yet steeling himself to do what he must. Here is what has become of the Othello of earlier acts—a man admirably self-possessed, the master of the situation. In this soliloquy, there are no references to strumpets or whores, nor to coupling goats or monkeys, nor to any other images which once racked him with jealousy. No longer is he possessed with revenge for his grievously injured pride. There remains, however, a passionate conviction of righteousness in his words—despite his monumental error.

He is convinced that he is being merciful in performing a deed that must be done. Thus he will not shed Desdemona's blood (instead, he will smother her); nor will he scar her physical beauty; nor would he, as we learn later, kill her *soul.* Yet he *will* kill her; Desdemona must die, "else she'll betray more men" (6). And there is devastating irony as he says, "Put out the light, and then put out the light" (7); Desdemona was once the "light" of his life and, also, light is often equated in Elizabethan dramas with reason, especially right reason, the aim of all men. Here, however, Othello means to act righteously, but he fails to use his sense of logic or reason; he has condemned Desdemona without proof, without reason. He is torn between his love for her (evidenced by his kiss) and his resolve to accomplish justice. Desdemona is a "pattern of excelling nature" (11), yet she is also "cunning" (11). He compares her to a rose which, once plucked, can bloom no more and must wither. For a moment, his love for her almost persuades "justice" (meaning Othello) "to break [his] sword" (17). He weeps, but he regains his purpose; Desdemona's beauty is deceptive, he realizes, because it masks her corruption.

When Othello's words awaken Desdemona, she begins an agonizing attempt to reason with her husband. The Moor then urges her to pray for forgiveness of any sin within her soul, and she becomes increasingly terrified. This he mistakenly concludes to be additional evidence of her guilt. He is as convinced of this as she is convinced that Othello is absolutely serious about killing her. Logically, she knows that she should have no cause for fear—she has done no wrong—yet she fears her husband.

Othello is not moved in the least by her insistence that she did not give the handkerchief to Cassio. And it is notable throughout this harrowing episode that Othello's language is controlled and elevated. As Desdemona cries out, first for heaven to have mercy on her and later for God Himself to have mercy on her, Othello voices a solemn "amen" to her prayers and addresses her as a "sweet soul" (50). Even now he refuses to see her as anything but a "perjur'd woman" (63) (a lying woman), one who forces him "to do / A murder" (64–65). At this moment, the motive of personal revenge surfaces again within him and replaces controlled justice. His resolve of self-control breaks when Desdemona calls out for Cassio; he is convinced that he indeed heard Cassio laughing about a sexual liaison with Desdemona. When Desdemona hears that Iago has killed Cassio, her self-control likewise vanishes. She pleads for her life, asking for banishment, asking for at least a day's stay in her execution, at least half a day, but she is overpowered by the Moor. He smothers her as she begs to say one last prayer.

It is at this moment that Emilia arrives outside the door, crying loudly for Othello. The Moor does not answer immediately. From his words, we realize that he is convinced that he is being merciful, if cruel, and that he intends to be sure that his wife is dead. The monstrosity of what he has done overwhelms him. Significant are lines 100–102, in which he says that there should be now "a huge eclipse / Of sun and moon"—that is, some evidence in the heavens that should acknowledge that the natural order of things has been grossly upset, that Desdemona is dead.

Again, Emilia calls out to Othello and, on entering, she shrieks about "foul murders" (106). Othello fears she is right and blames the moon, which "makes men mad" (111). It is then that he learns that Cassio lives, and he hears Desdemona's weak voice. Once more the young wife proclaims her innocence and insists that no one but herself is to blame. Indeed, she jeopardizes her very soul by deliberately lying in order to protect Othello, her husband, to whom she asks to be commended.

At first, Othello denies having any part in his wife's death. But then he loudly denounces her as a "liar, gone to burning hell" (129), admitting that he killed her. "She turn'd to folly, and she was a whore" (132); "she was false as water . . . Cassio did top her" (134–136). His proof is "honest, honest Iago" (154). Without hesitation, Emilia denounces Iago as a liar and Othello as a deceived "dolt" (163). She defies Othello's sword to right the injustice of this murder, vowing to "make thee known / Though I lost twenty lives" (165–166) and crying out for help, proclaiming that Othello has murdered Desdemona.

When Montano, Gratiano, and the others enter, Emilia challenges her husband to disprove what Othello has told her. In response to her pointed questions, Iago concedes that he did report that Desdemona was unfaithful, but that Othello himself found the same to be true. Summoning new courage, Emilia ignores her husband's command to be quiet and go home. Imploring the others to hear her, she curses Iago and prophetically states that perhaps she will never go home (197). All this finally becomes unbearable for the Moor, and he falls upon his wife's bed, only to be mocked by Emilia for his anguish. Gratiano then speaks and tells us that he finds comfort in the fact that Desdemona's father is not alive to hear of this tragedy; already he is dead of grief because of Desdemona's marrying the Moor.

Othello insists here that "Iago knows" (210) and, as further proof, he speaks of the handkerchief. At the mention of this, Emilia cries out again, this time appealing to God: No one will stop her now. She pays no attention to Iago's drawn sword as she tells how she found the handkerchief and gave it to Iago; she repeats her claim, even though Iago denounces her as a "villainous whore" (229) and a "liar" (231).

Thus the full truth is unfolded for Othello. He dashes toward Iago, is disarmed by Montano, and in the confusion, Iago kills Emilia, then flees. All leave, except the dying Emilia and the Moor, who can only berate himself. Emilia, aware that she is near death, recalls Desdemona's prophetic "Willow Song," a bit of which she sings. She reaffirms the innocence of her mistress just before she dies and concludes: "She lov'd thee, cruel Moor" (249).

Othello finds one of his prized weapons, a Spanish sword, and he recalls that he used the sword boldly in the past. Now, however, he has come to his "journey's end" (267). He sees himself as a lost soul—"where should Othello go?" (271). He is a "cursed slave" (276) who deserves the worst of punishment.

Lodovico, Montano, Iago (a prisoner now), and several officers enter; Cassio, in a chair, is brought in. The final moment of revelation is at hand. Othello lunges at Iago, wounds him, and is disarmed. Death is too good for Iago, he says; "'tis happiness to die" (290). Death is a relief he would not offer to his arch enemy. When Cassio states quietly that he never gave the Moor reason to distrust him, Othello readily accepts his word and asks for his pardon. Othello is freshly aware that he has been ensnared body and soul by "that demi-devil" (301) Iago, who refuses to confess his villainy. Lodovico then produces two letters found on Roderigo's body: one tells of the plan to slay Cassio, and the other is Roderigo's denunciation of Iago. The details of how Cassio obtained the handkerchief are revealed, and Othello bewails the fact that he has been a "fool! fool! fool!" (323).

Lodovico vows to punish Iago and tells Othello that he must return with him to Venice. Othello acknowledges the sentence, but before he is led away, he speaks his final lines. Unmistakably he has recovered his basic nobility and that gift of impressive language which he commanded so well prior to Iago's temptation.

Othello reminds his listeners of his past service to the Venetian state and pleads that his story shall be reported accurately so that all will know him *not* as a barbarous foreigner but as one who "lov'd not wisely but too well" (334), as one who was preyed upon and became "perplex'd in the extreme" (346) and "threw a pearl away / Richer than all his tribe" (347–348). We should not overlook this simile; Othello compares himself to the "base Judean" who threw away the most valuable pearl in the world. Relentless in his self-reproach, Othello tacitly compares himself to "a malignant and a turban'd Turk" (353); then, finished, he stabs himself in an attempt to atone for all that has happened. He chooses to execute the necessary justice upon himself. As he is dying, he says that he kissed Desdemona before he killed her. This suggests that perhaps his love for her flickered briefly within his dark soul before he murdered her. He reminds himself that perhaps he was not wholly corrupt, but he dies knowing that his soul is lost.

Lodovico's sad words end the tragedy. The sight of Othello, slumped against Desdemona's bed, "poisons sight" (364). He asks for the curtains to be drawn, for Gratiano to administer the Moor's estate, and for Iago to be punished. He must return to Venice and "with heavy heart" (371) relate "this heavy act" (371).

Glossary

minister (8) a servant.

Promethean heat (12) divine fire.

relume (13) relight.

forfend (32) forbid.

chrysolite (146) topaz; a gemstone.

reprobation (210) rejection by God.

liberal as the north (221) freely as the north wind blows.

stones (221) thunderbolts.

whipster (245) a term of contempt.

seamark (269) a beacon, destination.

compt (274) accounting on Judgment Day.

Judean (348) a possible reference to Judas Iscariot.

Spartan dog (362) a bloodhound.

CHARACTER ANALYSES

Othello

Othello is a combination of greatness and weakness, in his own words "an honourable murderer" (V.2, 295). He is a general in the Venetian defense forces, and, although a foreigner from Africa, he has won this post by excellence in the field of war. He has courage, intelligence, the skill of command, and the respect of his troops. Under pressure, he makes an inspiring speech. When the colony of Cyprus is threatened by the enemy, the Duke and Senate turn to "valiant" Othello to lead the defense.

After many years on campaign, Othello has come to live in Venice, among the sophisticated people of the city. Senator Brabantio has invited him to his home, and this is a revelation to the soldier. He is dazzled by the comfortable life, the learned conversation, the civilization. He appoints a student of military knowledge, Cassio, to be his lieutenant. Suddenly he sees possibilities for himself to which he had never before aspired.

Othello is an outsider who is intelligent and confident in military matters but socially insecure. He leads an intense life, swinging between triumph and dread. He is different from those around him, due to his origins and his life history, but he shares their religion, values, and patriotism to Venice. More importantly, he is visibly different due to the color of his skin, so he lives constantly among, but separated from, other people. Whenever they look at his black face, however brilliant a general he is, he knows the others are thinking "Yes, but he is not really one of us." Shakespeare presents this fact in the dialogue and also in the staging of the play: Othello's is a black face among a sea of white faces, and he is constantly referred to as "The Moor," a representative African, while others go by their personal names and are seen as independent individuals. When other characters call him "black," they refer to his face but also to the concept of color symbolism in Elizabethan morality: White is honor, black is wickedness; white is innocence, black is guilt.

Othello tells his life story to Desdemona, and she sees him through his words. The life of early separation from home and family, followed by danger and adventure, is perhaps the life story of thousands of men down the ages who become soldiers of fortune and who end up as corpses in ditches at an early age, unwept, unpaid, and unrecorded. Othello's achievement is not so much that he survived this unpromising life, but that he survived it in such a spectacularly successful manner, ending up one of the most powerful men in the Venetian defense forces.

On the field of battle Othello is skilled and triumphant; in the drawing room he is reluctant until Desdemona takes the lead and encourages him to tell his life story. It is Desdemona, as well as Othello, who turns the secret marriage into a social success with her skillfully worded defense.

Othello feels that his marriage is at the pinnacle of his life: "If it were now to die, / 'Twere now to be most happy, for I fear / My soul hath her content so absolute, / That not another comfort, like to this / Succeeds in unknown fate" (II.1, 190–194). He is triumphant in war and in love, the hero at his greatest moment. Such triumph, in a tragedy, cannot last.

Othello is aware of the precarious nature of success and happiness. "But I do love thee, and when I love thee not, / Chaos is come again" (III.3, 91–93). These are the words of a man who knows chaos and believes himself to have been rescued from it by love. Love for Othello puts order, peace, and happiness into his mental world, which would otherwise lapse back into chaos. He has grown up in exile, slavery, danger, and despair, now, as a professional soldier, he lives amongst chaos on the battlefield, but he need no longer have it in his inner being, because he has love. Chaos is the old concept of Hell, where everything is dreadful anguish, and Desdemona is the angel who has rescued Othello with her love.

When faced with the prospect of managing love and marriage, Othello's inexperience undermines his confidence. Iago finds it easy to drive Othello to jealousy and think that Desdemona loves another man because he already feels that her love for him is too good to be true. Othello sees Cassio as the man most Venetian women in Desdemona's position would like to marry and, therefore, as the man she would turn to if she ceased to love her husband. In a way, he is waiting for the dream to come to an end, for Desdemona to decide that she has made a mistake in marrying him.

Othello's insecurities are so close to the surface that a few words of hint and innuendo from Iago can tear the confident exterior and expose his fears, desires, and tendency to violence. Othello cannot stand uncertainty; it drives him to destroy his sanity. However, once he makes a decision, he is again the military man, decisive in action. Iago has only to push Othello to the belief that he has been betrayed, and Othello does the rest, judging, condemning, and executing Desdemona.

Fate is cruel to Othello, like the cruel fate of ancient Greek tragedies. Like the Greek heroes, Othello can confront this fate only with the best of his humanity. In his final speeches, Othello brings again a flash of his former greatness: his military glory, his loyalty to Venice, the intensity of his love, and his terrible realization that, by killing Desdemona, he has destroyed the best in himself. No man has full control over his life, but a man can judge himself and perform the execution and die with his love.

Iago

Shakespeare presents Iago as a collection of unsolvable puzzles. Each thing Iago says is cause for worry. He claims a reputation for honesty and plain speaking, yet he invents elaborate lies in order to exploit and manipulate other people. He treats others as fools and has no time for tender emotion, yet he is a married man and presumably once loved his wife. He cares for no one, yet he devotes his whole life to revenge rather than walk away in disdain. He believes in cheating and lying for gain, yet Shakespeare placed some of the most beautiful words in Iago's mouth.

Iago has a reputation for honesty, for reliability and direct speaking. Othello and others in the play constantly refer to him as "honest Iago." He has risen through the ranks in the army by merit and achievement, and Othello, whose military judgment is excellent, has taken him as *ancient* (captain) because of his qualities. In Iago, Shakespeare shows us a character who acts against his reputation. Possibly Iago was always a villain and confidence trickster who set up a false reputation for honesty, but how can one set up a reputation for honesty except by being consistently honest over a long period of time? Alternatively he might be a man who used to be honest in the past, but has decided to abandon this virtue.

Shakespeare has built the character of Iago from an idea already existing in the theatrical culture of his time: the Devil in religious morality plays, which developed into the villain in Elizabethan drama and tragedy. Iago says (I.1, 65) "I am not what I am," which can be interpreted as "I am not what I seem." But it is also reminiscent of a quotation from the Bible which Shakespeare would have known: In Exodus, God gives his laws to Moses on Mt. Sinai, and Moses asks God his name. God replies: "I am that I am" (Exodus,iii,14). If "I am that I am" stands for God, then Iago's self-description, "I am not what I am" is the direct opposite. Iago is the opposite of God, that is, he is the Devil. Iago in this play, has the qualities of the Devil in medieval and Renaissance morality plays: He is a liar, he makes promises he has no intention of keeping, he tells fancy stories in order to trap people and lead them to their destruction, and he sees other's greatest vulnerabilities and uses these to destroy them. Iago does all this not for any good reason, but for love of evil.

Iago is surrounded with bitter irony: he is not as he seems, his good is bad for others, people repeatedly rely on him, and he betrays them. He likes to have others unwittingly working to serve his purposes. But for all this, as his plot against Othello starts moving and gathering momentum, he loses control of it and must take real risks to prevent it from crashing. Iago is a man with an obsession for control and power over others who has let this obsession take over his whole life. Necessity forces his hand, and, in order to destroy Othello, he must also destroy Roderigo, Emilia, Desdemona, and ultimately himself. The one man who survived Iago's attempt to kill him, Cassio, is the only major character left standing at the end of the play.

William Hazlitt wrote: "Iago is an extreme instance . . . of diseased intellectual activity, with the most perfect indifference to moral good or evil, or rather with a decided preference of the latter, because it falls more readily in with his favorite propensity, gives greater zest to his thoughts and scope to his actions. He is quite or nearly indifferent to his own fate as to that of others; he runs all risks for a trifling and doubtful advantage, and is himself the dupe and victim of ruling passion—an insatiable craving after action of the most difficult and dangerous kind."

The great nineteenth-century actor Booth wrote about playing Iago: "To portray Iago properly you must seem to be what all the characters think, and say, you are, not what the spectators know you to be; try to win even them by your sincerity. Don't act the villain, don't look it, or speak it, (by scowling and growling, I mean), but think it all the time. Be genial, sometimes jovial, always gentlemanly. Quick in motion as in thought; lithe and sinuous as a snake."

Desdemona

Desdemona is a lady of spirit and intelligence. For all the claims of military straightforwardness of some other characters, Desdemona is the most direct and honest speaker in the play. Her speeches are not as lengthy as those of the men, but with Desdemona, every word counts.

For Desdemona, Othello is the hero of many exciting and dangerous adventures, who also has the appeal of the orphan child who needs love. Add to this the fact that he is now an honored and powerful man in her country, and what young noble woman would not find him attractive? As the Duke says, "I think this tale would win my daughter too" (I.3, 171).

In Cyprus, in charge of her own household, Desdemona continues to fulfil her duties, receiving petitioners as the commander's wife and being hostess at official receptions. Her marriage has brought her position and happiness, so much so that she finds it unbearable to think that her husband has turned against her. This numbness lasts until she sees that he actually intends to kill her; then she puts up a brave and spirited defense, insisting on her innocence. In despair at losing his love, she still defends him from the consequences of his actions, but he is past seeing what is clear to her and to Shakespeare's audience: that she has committed herself wholly to loving him; without his love, she cannot live.

Emilia

Emilia is Iago's wife, and Desdemona's maid, a woman of practical intelligence and emotional resilience. She follows Iago in wifely duty, but during the play develops a strong loyalty to Desdemona and, at the end, denounces Iago's lies to defend Desdemona's reputation. She speaks disparagingly of men, but, until the last scene, she supports her husband when needed. When finally she sees the truth, Emilia abandons all loyalty to Iago and verbally attacks him for the villain he is. In response, he silences her by killing her. She believes most men are foolish, wicked, or perverse, and nothing she experiences during the course of the play disproves that assessment.

CRITICAL ESSAYS

Character Pairs

Many of the scenes in Othello work by the pairing of two characters who are basically different in values or hidden agendas, putting them together through an experience or event, which has a different significance for each. Such pairs are Iago and Roderigo, Desdemona and Emilia, Othello and Iago, and Iago and Emilia.

Iago is paired with Roderigo for purposes of exploitation. By talking to him, Iago can show the audience his wicked intentions, yet Roderigo is so gullible that he is an easy dupe. Desdemona and Emilia are newly in each other's company, but quickly develop a friendly style of conversation that contrasts their different approaches to life. Emilia is down to earth to Desdemona's nobility, and practical to Desdemona's romanticism. Yet, when a crisis comes, they both share the same basic values of honesty and loyalty.

Iago and Emilia, although married and appearing to be similar personalities on the surface, see the world differently. Iago has the reputation of the "rough diamond," who speaks directly and honestly, but he uses his reputation as a disguise for his plotting, whereas the "rough diamond" really is Emilia's true nature. Their conversations are oppositions of opinion about the nature of men or women, or attempts by Iago to control Emilia's actions, balanced—until she discovers his true nature—by Emilia's willingness to do things to please her husband.

The development of the Othello-Desdemona pair is more hidden, and more complex. There is a polite formality of words between these two which persists below the endearments of the first half and the abuse and anguish of the second. At a certain level, they always treat each other as respected strangers, and as circumstances drive them apart, only this formal politeness remains as a frame for communication in the final act, where they go in different emotional directions, despite their underlying love for each other.

Major Themes

A theme in a literary work is a recurring, unifying subject or idea, a motif that allows us to understand more deeply the character and their world. In *Othello,* the major themes reflect the values and the motivations of the characters.

Love

In *Othello,* love is a force that overcomes large obstacles and is tripped up by small ones. It is eternal, yet derailable. It provides Othello with intensity but not direction and gives Desdemona access to his heart but not his mind.

Othello takes Desdemona to Cyprus, the ancient dwelling place of Aphrodite, the Greek goddess of love. But Othello's Cyprus is fortified and dedicated to war, and love has lost its supremacy. Othello believes he is now devoted to love, but by consistently putting war first, he has slighted Aphrodite, and so, although he is victorious in battle, he is defeated in love.

Othello finds that love in marriage needs time to build trust, and his enemy works too quickly for him to take that time. The immediate attraction between the couple works on passion, and Desdemona builds on that passion a steadfast devotion whose speed and strength Othello cannot equal. Yet even his secret enemy, Iago, sees his constant and noble nature and judges that he will "prove to Desdemona a most dear husband." Hating Othello, Iago sets out to prevent that happening.

Iago often falsely professes love in friendship for Roderigo and Cassio and betrays them both. Desdemona's love in friendship for Cassio is real but is misinterpreted by the jealous Othello as adulterous love. The true love in friendship was Emilia's for Desdemona, shown when she stood up to witness for the honor of her dead mistress, against Iago, her lying husband, and was killed for it.

Iago uses the word "love" in a wider and falser manner than the other characters. He tells Roderigo he loves him at moments when he is deceiving him, getting at his money, or persuading him to a course of action from which Iago, not Roderigo, will benefit. Iago tells Othello he loves him at moments when he is whispering the cruelest words into his ear. Iago even says he loves Desdemona, meaning he could feel some sexual desire for her. Iago cannot say "love" honestly: For Iago, love is leverage.

Prejudice

Iago's scheme would not have worked without the underlying atmosphere of racial prejudice in Venetian society, a prejudice of which both Desdemona and Othello are very aware. Shakespeare's Desdemona copes with prejudice by denying it access to her own life: Her relationship with Othello is one of love, and she is deliberately loyal only to that.

Othello, however, is not aware how deeply prejudice has penetrated into his own personality. This absorbed prejudice undermines him with thoughts akin to "I am not attractive," "I am not worthy of Desdemona," "It cannot be true that she really loves me," and "If she loves me, then there must be something wrong with her." These thoughts, inflamed by Iago's hints and lies, prevent Othello from discussing his concerns and fears directly with Desdemona, and so he acts on panicked assumption. In order to survive the combined onslaught of internalized prejudice and the directed venom of Iago, Othello would have had to be near perfect in strength and self-knowledge, and that is not a fair demand for anyone.

Jealousy

Jealousy is what appears to destroy Othello. It is the emotion suggested to him by Iago, when he says, "O beware jealousy; / It is the green ey'd monster, which doth mock / That meat it feeds on" (III.3, 169–170). Iago thinks he knows jealousy, having rehearsed it in his relationship with Emilia to the extent that Emilia believes jealousy is part of the personality of men, but Iago's jealousy is a poor, weak thing compared to the storm of jealousy he stirs up in Othello.

Iago has noticed Othello's tendency to insecurity and overreaction, but not even Iago imagined Othello would go as far into jealousy as he did. Jealousy focuses Othello's mind so tightly on one idea, the idea that Desdemona has betrayed him with Cassio, that no other assurance or explanation can penetrate. Such an obsession eclipses Othello's reason, his common sense, and his respect for justice.

Up to the moment he kills Desdemona, Othello's growing jealousy maddens him past the recall of reason. Upon seeing that she was innocent and that he killed her unjustly, Othello recovers. He can again see his life in proportion and grieve at the terrible thing he has done. Once again, he speaks with calm rationality, judging and condemning and finally executing himself.

Appearance and Reality

Appearance and reality are important aspects in *Othello*. For Othello, seeing is believing, and proof of the truth is visual. To "prove" something is to investigate it to the point where its true nature is revealed.

Othello demands of Iago "Villain, be sure thou prove my love a whore, be sure of it, give me the ocular proof" (III.3, 365–366).

What Iago gives him instead is imaginary pictures of Cassio and Desdemona to feed his jealousy. As Othello loses control of his mind, these pictures dominate his thoughts. He looks at Desdemona's whiteness and is swept up in the traditional symbolism of white for purity and black for evil. Whenever he is in doubt, that symbolism returns to haunt him, and despite his experience, he cannot help but believe it.

The significance of red is love, red strawberries like red hearts on the love token handkerchief, and like the red stains from Othello and Desdemona's first night of love on the marriage sheets. Such red on white is private and dear to the heart of Othello, and he expects it to be similarly dear to his wife. It is the belief that Desdemona gave away his handkerchief that drives him to kill her.

Honesty, Falseness, and Christian Values

All the characters in Othello work within a context of background assumptions of traditional Christian values, which center on the concepts of honesty and sexual morality. In the world of Othello, an honest person is straightforward and reliable, tells the truth when it is appropriate to speak, and keeps silent on occasion. Honesty involves keeping one's word about what one will do or say and remaining constant to one's loyalties. An honest person is reliable in social and business matters, is a loyal friend, and can be trusted to keep a secret. Furthermore, an honest person is assumed to be reliable in terms of sexual morality. Sexual morality involves fidelity in marriage and abstinence outside marriage. Human nature being as it is, such an ideal is not always reached, and there is wide room in Shakespeare's society, thought, and language for adultery, prostitution, and impulsive words and actions later regretted.

The opposite of "honest," meaning either "reliable" or "sexually correct," is "false," with its connotations of counterfeit, unreliable, bad, and rotten. Sexually correct behavior is "chaste," incorrect behavior is "unchaste." Othello kills Desdemona because he thinks she is false, and Iago kills Emilia because she is honest.

In the world of *Othello,* these values are upheld as the basis for acceptable social interaction, and although the play is built around values founded in Christianity, there is very little religious awareness and concern in the dialogue, the exception being in the murder scene, where Othello proposes giving Desdemona time to pray for forgiveness of her sins before she dies. Desdemona, however, is far more concerned with talking Othello out of killing her and says only a very general "Lord have mercy on me." Iago never shows any concern for the values he abuses, but treats his life as a matter for cunning, maneuvering within his immediate environment only.

Shakespeare's Tragedy

The dramatic form of classical tragedy derives from the tragic plays of ancient Athens, which depicted the downfall of a hero or famous character of Greek legend. The hero would struggle against overwhelming fate, and his defeat would be so noble that he wins the moral victory over the forces that destroy him. A tragedy evoked pity and terror in the audience; it was a catharsis, or washing clean of the soul, which left the spectator trembling but purified.

Unity, Time, and Place

Aristotle proposed the tragic unities of Place, Time, and Action, that is, the whole tragedy would take place in a single location, for example a house or a city square (this included messengers who came in from elsewhere), it would happen during the course of one day (including speeches about events which had happened in the past), and it would be a single story, without sub-plots.

Compared with these strict rules, Shakespeare's tragedy is a more relaxed genre, but *Othello* much more than, for example, the sprawling *Hamlet,* observes the spirit of Aristotle. Othello, apart from Act I in Venice, is located entirely within the fortress at Cyprus. Although logically the play covers an unspecified time lapse of, we presume, two or three weeks, it proceeds, more or less, by major scenes through the hours of the day, starting in Venice with the elopement after midnight, the Senate meeting at dawn, then at Cyprus with the morning storm and afternoon landings and developments, the fateful drinking party in the early evening and the murder at bed time. This is not to say that everything happens in the same day; it obviously cannot, but the impression is of an abstract day unfolding.

The plot is fairly unified, focusing on Othello and his fate, and dealing with other people and events only in so far as they are relevant to this focus. Othello is about as near as Shakespeare gets to classical tragedy.

The Tragic Flaw

A. C. Bradley saw Shakespearean tragedy characterized by the "tragic flaw," the internal imperfection in the hero that brings him down. His downfall becomes his own doing, and he is no longer, as in classical tragedy, the helpless victim of fate. Some say that Othello's tragic flaw was jealousy which flared at suspicion and rushed into action unchecked by calm common sense. A more modern interpretation would say that Othello's tragic flaw was that he had internalized, that is taken into himself, the prejudices of those who surrounded him. In his heart he had come to believe what they believed: that a black man is an unattractive creature, not quite human, unworthy of love. Thinking this, he could not believe that Desdemona could truly love him for himself. Her love must be a pretense, or a flawed and corrupted emotion. Iago hinted at these ideas, and Othello rushed to accept them, because they echoed his deepest fears and insecurities.

The Play's Structure

Shakespearean tragedy usually works on a five-part structure, corresponding to the five acts: Part One, the exposition, outlines the situation, introduces the main characters, and begins the action. Part Two, the development, continues the action and introduces complications. Part Three, the crisis (or climax), brings everything to a head. In this part, a change of direction occurs or understanding is precipitated. Part Four includes further developments leading inevitably to Part Five, in which the final crisis of action or revelation and resolution are explained. Othello follows this pattern.

CliffsNotes Review

Use this CliffsNotes Review to test your understanding of the original text, and reinforce what you've learned in this book. After you work through the review and essay questions, identify the quote section, and the fun and useful practice projects, you're well on your way to understanding a comprehensive and meaningful interpretation of *Othello*.

Q&A

1. Why has Roderigo been paying Iago large sums of money?_____

2. Iago claims he's angry with Othello for

   a. passing him over for a promotion

   b. marrying Desdemona

   c. planning on going to Cyprus without him

3. Iago slips away so quickly after he and Roderigo have alerted Brabantio that Desdemona has eloped because

   a. Brabantio dislikes him

   b. his wife expects him home

   c. he needs to continue the ruse of "loving" Othello

4. Iago's first success in making Othello believe that Desdemona and Cassio are lovers occurs when

   a. Iago mentions Desdemona's lost handkerchief

   b. Iago and Othello see Cassio hurriedly leave Desdemona

   c. Iago talks with Cassio about Bianca

5. Identify the "green ey'd monster." _____

6. Describe the handkerchief that Desdemona loses.

   a. it's monogrammed with the initials of Othello's family

   b. it's rare embroidered silk that Othello brought back from one of his many campaigns

   c. It has a pattern of strawberries on it

7. How does Othello die?

a. he stabs himself

b. Lodovico kills him in a rage upon finding Desdemona dead

c. he doesn't die; he's taken back to Venice to answer charges

Answers: (1) For Iago to woo Desdemona for him (2) a. (3) c. (4) b. (5) jealousy (6) c. (7) a.

Identify the Quote

1. I see this hath a little dash'd your spirits.

2. I think this tale would win my daughter too.

3. I do perceive here a divided duty.

4. You must not think, that I am drunk.

5. Nay, lay thee down and roar.

6. Put out the light, and then put out the light.

7. I am not what I am.

8. The more angel she, and you the blacker devil!

9. What is it that they do, when they change us for others?

10. A balmy breath, that doth almost persuade justice herself to break her sword.

Answers: (1) [Iago, after he has planted the suspicion in Othello's mind that Desdemona has been unfaithful (III.3, 217)] (2) [The Duke, after Othello tells how he won Desdemona's love by telling his life story (I.3, 171)] (3) [Desdemona, acknowledging before the Senators her duty to her father but stating that this duty is overridden by her duty to her husband (I.3, 181)] (4) [Cassio, when Iago has made him drunk so that Roderigo can goad him into a fight as an excuse to kill him (II.3, 112)] (5) [Emilia, when she realizes a villain has driven Othello to kill his wife (V.2, 199)] (6) [Othello, when he is about to kill Desdemona (V.2, 7)] (7) [Iago, telling Roderigo that he is a villain (I,1, 65)] (8) [Emilia, after the murder, when Othello confesses (V.2,132)] (9) [Emilia, on the faults of husbands (IV.3, 96)] (10) [Othello, hesitating as he is about to kill Desdemona (V.2, 16)]

Essay Questions

1. Describe the course of Iago's deception of Othello, showing which incidents were planned and which were opportunistic. Does Iago succeed by skill or by luck?

2. Discuss how age, social position, and race impact the relationship between Othello and Desdemona.

3. A tragedy concerns the fall of a great man due to some flaw in his character. What is Othello's flaw, and explain how he is truly a tragic hero.

4. What are possible motives for Iago's hatred of Othello? Consider both the motives he states and the motives implied in his speech and behavior.

5. In addition to exposing the prejudices of Venetians, discuss how the play also exposes the prejudices of the audience.

Practice Projects

1. Shakespeare's plays contain excellent speeches that can be worked up as audition pieces. Select a speech from the following list (or find another) and present it to your classmates:

> Iago (I,i,42–65). Iago explains that he is a villain.
>
> Othello (I,iii,128–170). His courtship of Desdemona.
>
> Desdemona (I,iii,180–189). I do perceive here a divided duty.
>
> Emilia (IV,iii,86–103). Husbands drive their wives to infidelity.
>
> Othello (V,ii,1–22). It is the cause, my soul.

2. Act the major scenes, spreading the roles around the group of students.

3. View a film (or theater) production of Othello and note and then discuss any differences. For example, in films, the script is often cut to simplify the story and to fit the play into a shorter time limit. Discuss the director's reasons for these cuts and the impact on the audience's reaction to the play.

CliffsNotes Resource Center

The learning doesn't need to stop here. CliffsNotes Resource Center shows you the best of the best—links to the best information in print and online about the author and/or related works. And don't think that this is all we've prepared for you; we've put all kinds of pertinent information at www.cliffsnotes.com. Look for all the terrific resources at your favorite bookstore or local library and on the Internet. When you're online, make your first stop www.cliffsnotes.com where you'll find more incredibly useful information about *Othello*.

Books

This CliffsNotes book, published by Wiley, provides a meaningful interpretation of *Othello*. If you are looking for information about the author and/or related works, check out these other publications:

Shakespeare, the Invention of the Human, by Harold Bloom, explores the impact Shakespeare has on the way people think. New York: Riverland Books, 1998.

The Western Canon, The Books and Schools of the Ages, by Harold Bloom, examines Shakespeare and Dante as the center of Western literature. New York: Harcourt Brace and Company, 1994.

Shakespearean Tragedy: Lectures on Hamlet, Othello, King Lear, and Macbeth, by A. C. Bradley, includes essays examining some of Shakespeare's most well-known tragedies. New York: St. Martin's Press, 1967.

The Arden Shakespeare: Othello, edited by M. R. Ridley, is an excellent annotated edition, with variants and notes. Cambridge, Mass.: Methuen Harvard, 1962.

The Portable Renaissance Reader, edited by James Bruce Ross and Mary Martin McLaughlin, includes essays on Renaissance history, politics, literature, theatre, culture, science, and philosophy. New York: Viking, 1953.

The New Cambridge Shakespeare: Othello, edited by Norman Sanders, is an excellent edition with notes on word meanings, Shakespeare's theater, and more. Cambridge, Mass: Cambridge University Press, 1984.

Shakespeare: Othello, edited by John Wain, includes 12 essays across the centuries. Part of the Casebook Series. London: MacMillan, 1971.

The Cambridge Companion to Shakespeare Studies, edited by Stanley Wells, offers 17 essays on all aspects of Shakespeare studies: biography, context, literature, productions, critical approaches, and more. Cambridge, Mass.: Cambridge University Press, 1986.

Shakespeare: the Evidence, by Ian Wilson, examines Shakespeare's life and plays in historical context. New York: St Martins Griffon, 1993.

It's easy to find books published by Wiley. You'll find them in your favorite bookstores (on the Internet and at a store near you). We also have three Web sites that you can use to read about all the books we publish:

- `www.cliffsnotes.com`
- `www.dummies.com`
- `www.wiley.com`

Internet

Check out these Web resources for more information about William Shakespeare and *Othello*:

Mr. William Shakespeare and the Internet, `http://daphne.palomar.edu/shakespeare/`—Despite its unwieldy title, this is the best meta-index for Shakespeare resources on the entire Web. From here, you can jump to just about anything that has to do with *Othello* in particular and Shakespeare's work in general.

Folger Shakespeare Library Home Page, `http://www.folger.edu/welcome.htm`— The Folger Shakespeare Library is a major center for scholarly research, housing the world's largest collection of Shakespeare's printed works, in addition to other rare Renaissance books and manuscripts. Teachers may find the Teaching Shakespeare link particularly helpful.

Shakespeare Web Home Page, http://www.shakespeare.com— An interactive discussion site dedicated to Shakespearean topics.

Next time you're on the Internet, don't forget to drop by www.cliffnotes.com. We created an online Resource Center that you can use today, tomorrow, and beyond.

Video

For a recent film production of Othello, check out the following film:

Othello. Dir. Oliver Park. Castle Rock. 1995. This film stars Laurence Fishburne as Othello, Kenneth Branagh as Iago, and Irene Jacob as Desdemona.

Send Us Your Favorite Tips

In your quest for knowledge, have you ever experienced that sublime moment when you figure out a trick that saves time or trouble? Perhaps you realized you were taking ten steps to accomplish something that could have taken two. Or you found a little-known workaround that achieved great results. If you've discovered a useful tip that gave you insight into or helped you understand *Othello* and you'd like to share it, the CliffsNotes staff would love to hear from you. Go to our Web site at www.cliffsnotes.com and click the Talk to Us button. If we select your tip, we may publish it as part of CliffsNotes Daily, our exciting, free e-mail newsletter. To find out more or to subscribe to a newsletter, go to www.cliffsnotes.com on the Web.

Index

NOTES

NOTES

CliffsNotes

LITERATURE NOTES

Absalom, Absalom!
The Aeneid
Agamemnon
Alice in Wonderland
All the King's Men
All the Pretty Horses
All Quiet on the
   Western Front
All's Well &
   Merry Wives
American Poets of the
   20th Century
American Tragedy
Animal Farm
Anna Karenina
Anthem
Antony and Cleopatra
Aristotle's Ethics
As I Lay Dying
The Assistant
As You Like It
Atlas Shrugged
Autobiography of
   Ben Franklin
Autobiography of
   Malcolm X
The Awakening
Babbit
Bartleby & Benito
   Cereno
The Bean Trees
The Bear
The Bell Jar
Beloved
Beowulf
The Bible
Billy Budd & Typee
Black Boy
Black Like Me
Bleak House
Bless Me, Ultima
The Bluest Eye & Sula
Brave New World
TheBrothers Karamazov

The Call of the Wild &
   White Fang
Candide
The Canterbury Tales
Catch-22
Catcher in the Rye
The Chosen
The Color Purple
Comedy of Errors...
Connecticut Yankee
The Contender
The Count of
   Monte Cristo
Crime and Punishment
The Crucible
Cry, the Beloved
   Country
Cyrano de Bergerac
Daisy Miller &
   Turn...Screw
David Copperfield
Death of a Salesman
The Deerslayer
Diary of Anne Frank
Divine Comedy-I.
   Inferno
Divine Comedy-II.
   Purgatorio
Divine Comedy-III.
   Paradiso
Doctor Faustus
Dr. Jekyll and Mr. Hyde
Don Juan
Don Quixote
Dracula
Electra & Medea
Emerson's Essays
Emily Dickinson Poems
Emma
Ethan Frome
The Faerie Queene
Fahrenheit 451
Far from the Madding
   Crowd
A Farewell to Arms
Farewell to Manzanar
Fathers and Sons
Faulkner's Short Stories

Faust Pt. I & Pt. II
The Federalist
Flowers for Algernon
For Whom the Bell Tolls
The Fountainhead
Frankenstein
The French
   Lieutenant's Woman
The Giver
Glass Menagerie &
   Streetcar
Go Down, Moses
The Good Earth
The Grapes of Wrath
Great Expectations
The Great Gatsby
Greek Classics
Gulliver's Travels
Hamlet
The Handmaid's Tale
Hard Times
Heart of Darkness &
   Secret Sharer
Hemingway's
   Short Stories
Henry IV Part 1
Henry IV Part 2
Henry V
House Made of Dawn
The House of the
   Seven Gables
Huckleberry Finn
I Know Why the
   Caged Bird Sings
Ibsen's Plays I
Ibsen's Plays II
The Idiot
Idylls of the King
The Iliad
Incidents in the Life of
   a Slave Girl
Inherit the Wind
Invisible Man
Ivanhoe
Jane Eyre
Joseph Andrews
The Joy Luck Club
Jude the Obscure

Julius Caesar
The Jungle
Kafka's Short Stories
Keats & Shelley
The Killer Angels
King Lear
The Kitchen God's Wife
The Last of the
   Mohicans
Le Morte d'Arthur
Leaves of Grass
Les Miserables
A Lesson Before Dying
Light in August
The Light in the Forest
Lord Jim
Lord of the Flies
The Lord of the Rings
Lost Horizon
Lysistrata & Other
   Comedies
Macbeth
Madame Bovary
Main Street
The Mayor of
   Casterbridge
Measure for Measure
The Merchant
   of Venice
Middlemarch
A Midsummer Night's
   Dream
The Mill on the Floss
Moby-Dick
Moll Flanders
Mrs. Dalloway
Much Ado About
   Nothing
My Ántonia
Mythology
Narr. ...Frederick
   Douglass
Native Son
New Testament
Night
1984
Notes from the
   Underground

The Odyssey
Oedipus Trilogy
Of Human Bondage
Of Mice and Men
The Old Man and
the Sea
Old Testament
Oliver Twist
The Once and
Future King
One Day in the Life of
Ivan Denisovich
One Flew Over the
Cuckoo's Nest
100 Years of Solitude
O'Neill's Plays
Othello
Our Town
The Outsiders
The Ox Bow Incident
Paradise Lost
A Passage to India
The Pearl
The Pickwick Papers
The Picture of
Dorian Gray
Pilgrim's Progress
The Plague
Plato's Euthyphro...
Plato's The Republic
Poe's Short Stories
A Portrait of the
Artist...
The Portrait of a Lady
The Power and
the Glory
Pride and Prejudice
The Prince
The Prince and
the Pauper
A Raisin in the Sun
The Red Badge of
Courage
The Red Pony
The Return of the
Native
Richard II
Richard III

The Rise of
Silas Lapham
Robinson Crusoe
Roman Classics
Romeo and Juliet
The Scarlet Letter
A Separate Peace
Shakespeare's
Comedies
Shakespeare's Histories
Shakespeare's
Minor Plays
Shakespeare's Sonnets
Shakespeare's Tragedies
Shaw's Pygmalion &
Arms...
Silas Marner
Sir Gawain...Green
Knight
Sister Carrie
Slaughterhouse-Five
Snow Falling on Cedars
Song of Solomon
Sons and Lovers
The Sound and the Fury
Steppenwolf &
Siddhartha
The Stranger
The Sun Also Rises
T.S. Eliot's Poems &
Plays
A Tale of Two Cities
The Taming of the
Shrew
Tartuffe, Misanthrope...
The Tempest
Tender Is the Night
Tess of the D'Urbervilles
Their Eyes Were
Watching God
Things Fall Apart
The Three Musketeers
To Kill a Mockingbird
Tom Jones
Tom Sawyer
Treasure Island &
Kidnapped
The Trial

Tristram Shandy
Troilus and Cressida
Twelfth Night
Ulysses
Uncle Tom's Cabin
The Unvanquished
Utopia
Vanity Fair
Vonnegut's Works
Waiting for Godot
Walden
Walden Two
War and Peace
Who's Afraid of
Virginia...
Winesburg, Ohio
The Winter's Tale
The Woman Warrior
Worldly Philosophers
Wuthering Heights
A Yellow Raft in
Blue Water

Check Out the All-New CliffsNotes Guides

TECHNOLOGY TOPICS

Balancing Your Check-
book with Quicken
Buying and Selling
on eBay
Buying Your First PC
Creating a Winning
PowerPoint 2000
Presentation
Creating Web Pages
with HTML
Creating Your First
Web Page
Exploring the World
with Yahoo!
Getting on the Internet
Going Online with AOL
Making Windows 98
Work for You

Setting Up a
Windows 98
Home Network
Shopping Online Safely
Upgrading and
Repairing Your PC
Using Your First iMac
Using Your First PC
Writing Your First
Computer Program

PERSONAL FINANCE TOPICS

Budgeting & Saving
Your Money
Getting a Loan
Getting Out of Debt
Investing for the
First Time
Investing in
401(k) Plans
Investing in IRAs
Investing in
Mutual Funds
Investing in the
Stock Market
Managing Your Money
Planning Your
Retirement
Understanding
Health Insurance
Understanding
Life Insurance

CAREER TOPICS

Delivering a Winning
Job Interview
Finding a Job
on the Web
Getting a Job
Writing a Great Resume